*If you're confused about which way to turn,*
*these books will point you in the right direction.*

## Books for Christian Living

### Stressed Out But Hangin' Tough
Andrea Stephens guides you in developing the skills you need to
cope with family strife, divorce, peer pressure, problems with your
girlfriend or boyfriend, school pressures, and other stresses that are
common to teens.

### Life, Sex, and Everything in Between
Each year Bill Sanders has the opportunity to speak to teens in
more than 150 high schools nationwide. In this book he tackles the
questions most asked by young people and provides sound
answers. Among the topics addressed here are safe sex, drug and
alcohol abuse, making or keeping friends, prayer, problems with
parents, and planning for the future.

## Devotions for Girls and Guys

### Prime Time
Bill and Andrea Stephens present fresh, relevant devotions that can
make the time you spend with God the best time of your day.

### Goalposts
These affirming devotions from Bill Sanders guide you in making
the right choices when temptations and distractions seem to
bombard you.

### Outtakes
Do you ever wonder how your belief in God really relates to what's
going on in your life? These devotions, written by Bill Sanders,
assure you that what matters most to you matters to God.

# GOD DOESN'T PLAY FAVORITES

 *Gutsy Devotions for Teens*

# William Coleman

 Fleming H. Revell
A Division of Baker Book House Co
Grand Rapids, Michigan 49516

Library of Congress Cataloging-in-Publication Data

Coleman, William L.
    God doesn't play favorites / William L. Coleman.
        p.    cm.
    Summary: A collection of devotional readings covering such topics as stress, attitude, heroism, and self-perception.
    ISBN 0-8007-5430-1
    1. Youth—Prayer-books and devotions—English.   [1. Prayer books and devotions.]   I. Title.
BV4571.2.C58    1992
242'.63—dc20                                                          91-33317
                                                                          CIP
                                                                          AC

Copyright © 1992 by William L. Coleman
Published by Fleming H. Revell
a division of Baker Book House Company
P.O. Box 6287, Grand Rapids, Michigan 49516-6287

ISBN: 0-8007-5430-1

Third printing, May 1993

Printed in the United States of America

*A Call on Your Machine . . .*

Every day there is a message for you on your spiritual telephone service. It's God, calling with some vital information and encouragement. Hopefully each of these chapters will help you keep in touch regularly with your loving Father.

# GOD
# DOESN'T
# PLAY
# FAVORITES

# ⭐ Good Ears ⭐

Why do most of us long for someone who will simply listen? Why do we need a person who will hear us out without:

> interrupting,
> giving advice,
> arguing,
> correcting,
> contradicting,
> judging,
> or any other form of rudeness?

Listening to someone is the ultimate compliment. Someone who listens says you are important, you are special, you have dignity, and you aren't just another bug on the windshield of life.

Good listeners are hard to find. Too many of us are in love with the sound of our own voices, so we talk instead of listen. Too many of us think we need to talk in order to feel important. So we fail to be patient and hear.

Among God's many gifts, he is a great listener. Equipped with good ears and a patient nature, God likes to hear what is going on with each of us.

Give ear to my words, O Lord, consider my sighing. Listen to my cry for help, my King and my God, for to you I pray. In the morning, O Lord, you hear my voice; in the morning I lay my requests before you and wait in expectation.

Psalm 5:1–3

9

# ☆ The Gift of Helping ☆

One evening a week Carol volunteered to answer calls on the local teen help line. Young people close to her age would call in to talk. Carol had a caring voice and a sincere heart, which made her perfect for the part.

Each evening she received questions on a wide range of subjects. Divorced parents, schoolwork, dating, depression, drugs, and even health were frequent topics. Because she had some training, Carol was able to make suggestions or else direct the caller to someone who could be of more help.

In most situations Carol felt comfortable trying to help people her own age. She didn't have to be Miss Know-Everything. More important, Carol was a good listener who loved people.

Helping others is something close to the heart of God. God could roam around the universe and not care what goes on down here, but he doesn't do that. Not only does God care, he also sets up a network of Christians who reach out to help one another.

Christian help should not be a constant cry, "How do I get help for myself?" A key ingredient of finding help is to give it to others. That's part of the divine plan.

If it is serving, let him serve; if it is teaching, let him teach; if it is encouraging, let him encourage; if it is contributing to the needs of others, let him give generously. . . .

Romans 12:7, 8

# ✭ No Favorites ✭

Teachers probably do have favorite students. If a young person has a clean face, decent clothes, and writes neatly, teachers are likely to find him appealing and acceptable. There isn't anything wrong with the teacher. Most of us react well to people who look fresh and alert.

Students who are not prepared and have a reputation for being slow in class probably are more difficult for a teacher to appreciate. Life can be hard, and some types of people are pushed to the back.

When a student is a minority race, doesn't play sports well, doesn't own good shoes, or has poor verbal skills, he is less likely to be anyone's favorite. These facts are sad, because many excellent, loving young people are left out in a crazy world of favorites.

Fortunately, there's great news for all of us: God doesn't play favorites. God loves boys with dirty faces and girls with stringy hair. He cares about young people who stumble on the baseball diamond as well as those who forget their homework. God loves the girls who get prom dates as well as the ones who stay home.

God simply doesn't have any favorites. He loves people of all colors, every social status, all talents, all incomes, and all reading abilities. He sent his Son to die for the student in the first row, the guy in the last row, and the befuddled teenager who didn't find his way to school at all today.

Then Peter began to speak: "I now realize how true it is that God does not show favoritism but accepts men and women from every nation who fear him and do what is right."

Acts 10:34, 35

# ☆ **Generous Teenagers** ☆

A couple of times a week Tami and Kathy went through the same routine. Before they left their fourth-hour class, each placed her cash on her desk, and they divided up whatever they had. Almost always Tami had less money than Kathy, and both of them knew it.

Playing the game, they divided their resources and then started for the cafeteria. Kathy normally had more money than she needed, and Tami was always just this side of bankruptcy. They enjoyed each other's company and frequently kidded about the way they shared.

Often they caught each other after school and went through the same routine in front of the soft-drink machine.

"Let's see how much we've got here." Kathy would dig into her small purse.

"Oh, I don't think I want anything," Tami would protest.

"Of course you do." Kathy held some change in her hand.

"I've got thirty-five cents," Tami said lamely.

"I've got the other sixty-five cents. Comes out perfect." Kathy began sliding coins into the slot.

Teenagers aren't necessarily the self-centered people they are made out to be. Those who follow Jesus Christ often learn that one of the first lessons of discipleship is how to develop a sharing attitude.

In everything I did, I showed you that by this kind of hard work we must help the weak, remembering the words the Lord Jesus himself said: "It is more blessed to give than to receive."

Acts 20:35

# ★ God's Sense of Humor ★

There is a chemistry test tomorrow and a history paper due Friday. Norm asks you out on a date and you would rather eat flies than go anywhere with that nerd. But how will you tell him no? And your parents expect you to work in the yard Saturday when everybody else is going to World of Thrills.

It's a lot of pressure and sometimes you think you might either fall apart or blow up. What is a person to do when everything feels like it is caving in?

You could try what God does. When God sees all kinds of stress mounting up, he merely takes time out and has a good laugh at it all.

God has a sharp sense of humor. Look at the funny-looking beetles he created. And how about lobsters and horseshoe crabs. God probably still gets a few chuckles out of them.

13

When the pressure mounts and everyone becomes upset at God, he stands back and laughs at the silly situation. God isn't likely to get an ulcer even if he could.

Don't let the stress tear you up. All stress passes sooner or later. If you can find the humorous side and laugh out loud, you can live a better life.

Our mouths were filled with laughter. . . .

Psalm 126:2

# ☆ His Grace Is Sufficient ☆

Three times a week Nate tied his gym shoes and got ready to be humiliated all over again. No matter what the schedule in his physical-education class, Nate knew he couldn't keep up.

If the class ran or climbed ropes, he couldn't do what everybody else seemed to handle with ease. When they played basketball, someone usually stole the ball from him. In touch football he was always told to block, and he didn't do that well.

Three times a week Nate spent fifty minutes feeling like a total dork. He could hardly wait to scurry back to history class, where he felt fairly comfortable.

Barely able to cope with the embarrassment, Nate eventually asked God to do him a huge favor. If Nate wasn't going to become a good athlete, he asked for a good attitude. He didn't want to become bitter.

God didn't make Nate the school quarterback who led the team to the state championship. But he did give ~~the~~ *him* ~~high school junior~~ a better attitude. He showed Nate how to appreciate and befriend other ~~teenagers~~ *young people* who had trouble with eye-hand coordination. God gave Nate the grace to turn his weakness into a strength by understanding others.

But he said to me, "My grace is sufficient for you, for my power is made perfect in weakness."

2 Corinthians 12:9

# ★ This Is a Big Day ★

There is something about today that makes it special. It's not the ball game or the party or the fact that you have a substitute teacher. Those are all circumstances that change and could make a day turn sour.

What makes this day great is that God has custom-made it. It will be like no other day you have ever lived. Use it well, because once this day passes off the calendar, it will never come back again. You can replace wheel covers, VCRs, and shoestrings, but each day rolls around only once.

Do you wonder what God had in mind by creating today? Maybe he wants you to meet someone new, or possibly he is going to put somebody in your path whom you could help—like the Good Samaritan. It could be that God wants to bring laughter into your life. Maybe he would like to strengthen you for some sorrow that will come later.

Did God put this day together so you could mend a relationship? This could turn out to be the perfect time to talk to God and tell him how you feel.

Today will be unique. There won't be another one exactly like it. Be smart and go out and make the most of it.

This is the day the Lord has made; let us rejoice and be glad in it.

Psalm 118:24

# ☆ Five-Minute Hero ☆

You will probably never swim across a raging river and climb a slippery bank to rescue some kidnapped children from a bamboo cage. The very thought of it may make you so tired you need to go get another piece of cake to calm your nerves.

You probably will not stop runaway horses or catch babies tossed from burning buildings. But for about five minutes, every once in a while, you can stand up and be a hero.

- Sometime you will see a young person being picked on, and you will go over and stand beside that person.

- One day in a pick-up football game you will hand the ball to someone who never gets it and say, "Here, you be quarterback."
- In a lunch room your eyes will see a depressed teenager sitting alone, and you will go over and join that person.
- A friend will tell you about a beer party in someone's basement and ask what you think. You will answer by explaining why that's a problem.

Five-minute heroes take a stand with someone else when they really need it. God gives us the faith and the strength to be dependable.

Therefore put on the full armor of God, so that when the day of evil comes, you may be able to stand your ground, and after you have done everything, to stand.

Ephesians 6:13

# ⭐ Getting Some Respect ⭐

Teen bashing is popular. Maybe it always has been. Someone is always talking about "dumb," "irresponsible," "reckless" teenagers. They make it sound as if youth is a disease and everyone who has it is sick or wacko.

There is a prejudice against teenagers in some circles. That's to be expected in a weird and unbalanced world.

The same distrust of youth existed when the Bible was written. The apostle Paul objected to youth bashing. He told young people to not let anyone look down on them. Instead they should show the complainers just how good young people can be.

Specifically, Paul said to zero in on these five areas, to silence many critics:

1. *Speech:* Don't try to shock and insult people.
2. *Life:* Conduct goes a long way toward creating trust.
3. *Love:* Treat others thoughtfully.
4. *Faith:* Attempt to follow Christ.
5. *Purity:* Make an effort to keep sin out.

Anyone who sees these five things in a teenager *ought* to give him plenty of respect.

Don't let anyone look down on you because you are young, but set an example for the believers in speech, in life, in love, in faith and in purity.

1 Timothy 4:12

# ★ Careful Whom You Lean On ★

Whom do young people go to when they want advice? Most teenagers go to other teenagers when they need someone to talk to. Usually it's a friend, but there are also organizations that make teenagers available to counsel other teenagers. Some schools have peer counseling programs. Some communities have telephone services where a teen can call another trained teen.

Such programs can literally be lifesavers. Almost all of us need a person to fill a special need in our lives once, twice, even many times. We get confused; the pressure gets us down, and we need someone to share with.

Leaning on people has become popular, and it should be encouraged. But we should take time to think twice before we pick a person to lean on. Some of our friends are rock, and they can be helpful. Others are like spiderwebs and will fail us when we try to lean on them.

Look for a Christian to lean on, if one can be found. If not, aim for someone with a strong value system. None of us want to be led into alcohol, drugs, or sex as a solution to very real problems.

Don't lean on just anyone when a storm hits. The cure might do more damage than the problem.

"What he trusts in is fragile; what he relies on is a spider's web. He leans on his web, but it gives way; he clings to it, but it does not hold."

Job 8:14, 15

# ⭐ Making Fun of Our Faith ⭐

Third period English class was almost always the same. No sooner had Jamie settled into his seat than Dave would turn around and say to him, "How's the deacon this morning? Save any souls yet today?"

Dave would then laugh with that little chipmunk sound and turn back around to face the chalkboard.

Almost every day Dave would ask the same two questions. The wording seldom changed.

Jamie began to tighten up after second period, because he knew what was waiting for him in the next hour. Sometimes he would resolve to tell Dave where to get off. Enough was enough, he decided, and someone should put this obnoxious bore in his place.

But for some reason Jamie held back. He tried hard to smile at irritating Dave, and the more he practiced, the easier it became. After a few weeks, Jamie began to kid Dave back in a gentle way.

Bless those who persecute you; bless and do not curse.

Romans 12:14

# ☆ **Put-down Artists** ☆

*Webster's* calls a put-down a humiliating remark. Sometimes put-downs are outrageously funny:

"Did you get a comic book with those shoes?"

"I bet a lot of rats had to die to make that coat."

"Those are great. Where can you buy glasses and a nose like that?"

"Good voice. Didn't I hear you on 'Wild Kingdom'?"

Put-downs are usually harmless trade-offs. Making fun of each other can be friendly as long as it doesn't cut too deeply or too close to what we think is important.

But put-downs have to be mixed with compliments and "put-ups." If we constantly thrash our friends, we start to make them feel terrible.

The Bible tells us to say good things, to make our friends feel better about themselves. Nobody wants to get slammed all the time.

Pleasant words are a honeycomb, sweet to the soul and healing to the bones.

Proverbs 16:24

# ✫ A Special Counselor ✫

Can you hear your conscience talking to you? It may not say words, but your conscience lets you know when something is right or wrong. Animals don't seem to have consciences. Mostly they do whatever their senses and instincts tell them. People are different. We make choices and bear responsibility on a higher level.

Too often we ignore our consciences and do whatever we want. That leads to trouble.

When you became a Christian, God sent a special counselor, called the Holy Spirit, to live inside you. He will be available to give advice, guidance, and even furnish courage when the choices are particularly tough.

Like our consciences, we can turn off the Holy Spirit if we don't want to listen. Most of us know how to ignore good advice and have frequently done that. But the Spirit of God is close, capable, and available when we want help.

But the Counselor, the Holy Spirit, whom the Father will send in my name, will teach you all things and will remind you of everything I have said to you.

John 14:26

# ✮ **The Other Side of Town** ✮

There is a great deal of prejudice between people with low incomes and those with high incomes. Some in the second group feel that people with little money must be shiftless, lazy, and have poor morals. At the same time some people with low incomes believe that anyone with money must have gotten it by cheating or by oppressing the poor.

When we judge people that way, we are showing prejudice toward them. We don't understand what people are like until we meet them, and even then we can't be exactly sure. The most important part of a person is character and not money. Integrity, fairness, and honesty tell us far more about a person than his car or his house or the clothes he wears.

Too often the first thing a parent or a teenager worries about is what side of town a person comes from. It's as if we could tell how good someone is by the size of his house.

As Christians we can know better than this. Jesus Christ collected disciples from both sides of town. Character and a heart for God were the great issues. Christ probably never asked a follower where he bought his tunic.

Live in harmony with one another. Do not be proud, but be willing to associate with people of low position. Do not be conceited.

Romans 12:16

# ⭐ Right and Wrong ⭐

There is a right and a wrong just as sure as there is a left and a right, an up and a down, a north and a south. If we tried to kill someone without any cause, that would be wrong. Killing people as if we were swatting flies is never right.

The same is true of stealing wives. If we meet a married woman and decide to try and win her away from her husband, that's wrong. We might try to make up an example in which wife stealing could be right, but deep inside we know better.

A couple of teenagers walked around the neighborhood on Halloween, taking candy from children who were out trick-or-treating. We could argue that the teenagers were doing the children a favor by fighting cavities and keeping their sugar count low. But we know it's wrong.

Sometimes it's hard to figure out what is right and wrong. Some things might be wrong, but then again. . . . That's one of the reasons God gave us the Bible. Its pages have great concepts on how to know what is right or just or fair or reasonable. The Bible doesn't tell us whether or not to chew gum in class or if we should paint our bedrooms purple. But it does help us grapple with the important moral decisions we need to handle.

The Bible gives us an idea of what God considers right and wrong.

. . . Acquiring a disciplined and prudent life, doing what is right and just and fair.

Proverbs 1:3

# ✭ Getting Off Alone ✭

Lucas got tired of being overrun with people. Someone was always in his bedroom, hanging around in his backyard, poking through his stuff. If it wasn't his friends, it was his family taking up his space.

It wasn't that Lucas disliked people. But having them around all the time left him on edge. Privacy was important to Lucas. He liked to think, to plan, to dream, even to talk to God.

He didn't want to tell people to buzz off, but he needed breathing space. As the problem grew worse, Lucas began to formulate a plan. On Thursday nights, when his parents bowled, he put a DO NOT DISTURB sign on his bedroom door, and if he was home alone, Lucas refused to answer the phone. Early every Tuesday evening he went to the public library and found a study room. For an hour he sat alone. He read. He thought. He prayed.

No recluse, Lucas was then able to go back and mix well with family and friends.

We don't like to ride the roller coaster all the time. Sometimes we like to sit alone in the park and get in touch with God. Nothing too formal, just a little time to level off.

It's worth the extra effort to find a place to be alone.

Once when Jesus was praying in private and his disciples were with him, he asked them, "Who do the crowds say I am?"

Luke 9:18

# ★ At War With Parents ★

The entire house seemed like a war zone to Rhonda. Her younger brother, Ben, was throwing paper planes in the family room. Out in the garage her father was steaming about something. Her mother was reading the newspaper, but she was ready to explode if anyone said the wrong thing.

As for herself, Rhonda sat in her room like a land mine. If anyone passed through the doorway, she was ready to blow up at him.

She wondered if family members should be issued army helmets. No one could be sure when flying tempers or shouting words might begin hitting the air.

Sometimes families get that way. Unfortunately a few families are that tense most of the time. Once in a while you meet a teenager who looks for ways to do battle at home.

Smart teenagers try to keep their cool and make peace with their parents. They have different life-styles and often different dreams, but that's no reason to war with parents. No matter how much young people want to be different, they still need to show respect for their parents. You can be one of these teens. Stay calm. Don't keep tossing hand grenades in the living room. If there is an occasional flare-up, try to make sure you didn't start it.

God's principle is still in use. We show respect and obedience for parents; we don't shoot rockets at them.

Children, obey your parents in the Lord, for this is right.

Ephesians 6:1

# ★ God Doesn't Do Facials ★

Sometimes women get redone. They have their hair whipped or sculpted into a different style. Or else they have their faces worked over for a new look. The cosmetologist experiments with new base creams or highlights or eye shadows. Women use wrinkle removers or freckle dimmers or a number of other beauty aids.

And for some it's worth all the effort. They may look great after getting made over.

God is interested in beauty, too, but not usually in the outside kind. Not that he wants us to look ugly, but most of God's beauty work is done on the inside.

> His job is to cheer up someone's heart.
> He specializes in producing forgiveness.
> His forte is highlighting love.
> He tries to bring out kindness.
> He is famous for creating generosity.
> He emphasizes thankfulness.

By tinkering with the inside, God helps make us into new and beautiful people. He lets other people work on split ends and stringy hair. He doesn't spend much time trying to disguise a double chin.

But when it comes to beauty that begins at the heart and sparkles out of the eyes, God is a first-class beautician.

Instead, [your beauty] should be that of your inner self, the unfading beauty of a gentle and quiet spirit, which is of great worth in God's sight.

1 Peter 3:4

# ✫ Recharged Batteries ✫

We have a flashlight that plugs into a wall socket. Like all flashlights, the batteries eventually run down, and we have to buy new ones. When we plug this flashlight into electricity, the batteries become recharged, and they will work for a much longer time.

God has given us a spiritual way to look at the world and the people in it. The way we treat people, our attitude toward greed, our desire to put others first, our drive to serve Jesus Christ, and many other values come from this spiritual outlook.

But spirituality, like flashlight batteries, has a way of running down. If we don't regularly plug in our spirituality, we soon have little at all. Then we forget about our dedication to Christ, our service to others, and our God-centered value system.

All of us have probably felt the drain. It's as if our lights are dull and our energy is low.

Christians can recharge in many ways. Some of the most familiar are by prayer, by Bible reading, and by surrender to the Holy Spirit. When we see that our spirituality is on a steady dim, we might become renewed by double-checking these three areas.

Do not conform any longer to the pattern of this world, but be transformed by the renewing of your mind.

Romans 12:2

# ★ Keep Us From Being Dweebs ★

A trained ear can pick out a dweeb from a distance of 65 feet in a crowd of 100 mixed teenagers. Dweebs come in most shapes and sizes. Their identifying marks are mostly vocal. A dweeb is someone who continuously says rude and obnoxious things.

Someone who slips up once in a while is not a dweeb. All of us are capable of occasional dweebisms. The true variety is distinguished by their repeatedly being rude and obnoxious.

Dweebs are so anxious to insult and degrade people that frequently they are heard before they are seen. When we hear a distant voice say, "Hey, wait up, sewer breath," we can be almost certain that a bona fide dweeb is about to come charging into view.

Potentially, dweebs are nice people. Mostly they are looking for attention and don't know a good way to get it. It is illegal to shoot dweebs, but they probably won't look good mounted over your mantle anyway.

God has a particular interest in changing dweebs into normal people. Part of the way he does that is to teach us to put the clamps on rude and obnoxious behavior. If attention is our goal, we can get it much better by saying kind and helpful things to as many people as possible.

Lord, deliver us from dweebism.

Let your conversation be always full of grace, seasoned with salt, so that you may know how to answer everyone.

Colossians 4:6

# ☆ Who Took My Books? ☆

Almost every morning the Spivak family heard the same question bellowing from the living room. "Hey, who took my books?"

Each time Mike said it, the rest of the family simply groaned and otherwise ignored him. Sometimes Phil, his brother, would answer with, "Oh, it must have been one of those infamous book gangs on the prowl again. They keep raiding homes and stealing schoolbooks."

"Knock it off, man," Mike would answer. "This isn't funny. My history homework was in there."

More often Mike's mother would say a kind word and help her son look for the missing books. "Well, where did you put them?" she would ask, looking under newspapers and cushions.

"I put them right here," said Mike. "But somebody must have taken them."

This little scene went on for years, with Mike always insisting that someone else lost his books. His first instinct was to blame others for his mistakes.

Blaming other people for our mistakes is the oldest game in history. After Adam sinned, God found him and asked what happened. Adam said he sinned because of the woman God sent to him. Nice try, Adam.

The first man tried to dump his mess-up on both God and his wife. Some of us are great at pushing the blame off on others, too.

The man said, "The woman you put here with me—she gave me some fruit from the tree, and I ate it."

Genesis 3:12

# ★ The Pressure Starts Early ★

The pressure for teenagers to date as early as possible is becoming enormous. Even preteens feel a need to go out with someone so their friends won't think they are social misfits.

Where does the pressure come from? Are young people really dying to be with someone of the opposite sex? Are thirteen-year-olds afraid life will pass them by if they don't find someone to go out with?

In most cases the pressure to date comes from two

sources. First, teens' friends think they should date. Peer pressure is as strong as any force a teenager can feel. Second, many parents want to see their children date as early as possible. They don't want to think of their children as left out of any fun. That's when parents begin to organize dances and parties where young people can take dates.

Pressure means someone is trying to get you to do something you don't want to do. If it were pressure to take medicine for your shrunken gall bladder, it might be all right. But other people trying to make you date someone before you're ready, that's a little goofy.

If a young person isn't ready to date, he shouldn't feel forced into it. There is a time for everything as there is a time to chill out and not hurry.

There is a time for everything, and a season for every activity under heaven.

Ecclesiastes 3:1

# ☆ **Who Knows What to Do?** ☆

Amanda said she couldn't help herself. When she attended classes, her friends would make fun of her. They had either half dropped out or completely stopped going to school. Now they wanted her to give up and join them.

She had a tough time knowing what to do. Half the time she wasn't sure what was right and what was wrong.

Eventually the constant pulling became too much, and Amanda gave up on her education.

The questions of right and wrong are hard to sift through. Read the paper, watch television, listen to friends, hear songs, and choices often become even harder to make.

We need some source that can give us a dependable idea of what to do and what to leave alone. The Bible supplies these basics to sound decision making. It won't tell us whether to mix plaids and stripes, but it will furnish great guidance for making moral decisions.

The Bible gives guidance in two ways. First, there are commands; God tells us not to get drunk and not to murder anyone. But second, it also offers good values. It tells us to hold down our anger and not make rash decisions and never cheat our bosses.

Like an island in the sea, the Bible is a great place to find solid ground. Without it we simply swim endlessly and are never quite sure where we are.

How can a young man keep his way pure? By living according to your word.

Psalm 119:9

# ★ When You Feel ★ Like Screaming

Have you ever felt your heart racing, your adrenaline pumping, and your face running hot? Have you ever wanted to run outside in the snow and scream at the top of your lungs? Have you ever thought you were a hot-air balloon that was blown up too large and about to pop?

If you have felt like this, you know what it's like to suffer from high anxiety. And you know it isn't any fun.

The Bible tells us we can trade off high anxiety for the peace of God. Peace doesn't come automatically. If we don't make a trade, it won't work.

We reduce our anxiety by increasing our praise and prayer to God. The formula goes like this:

Instead of worrying we talk to God:

1. We say what we want to happen.
2. We thank God for what he is already doing.

This won't remove all of our anxiety. We like to hold some of it back. Sometimes we will still feel like screaming in the backyard. But the formula helps us stay in balance.

Paul explained it this way:

Do not be anxious about anything, but in everything, by prayer and petition, with thanksgiving, present your requests to God. And the peace of God, which transcends all understanding, will guard your hearts and your minds in Christ Jesus.

Philippians 4:6, 7

# ✸ **Low-Grade Rebels** ✸

Even on the best of days Tracey found herself tossing a dozen or so dirty words around. She either cursed under her breath or occasionally threw out some choice words for public consumption.

Once in a while Tracey was startled at what she said. She became uneasy over what she might say next, if she didn't watch herself.

Two things were going on in her life. One was that cursing had become a habit. She said words when they were meaningless, even dumb. Also, Tracey understood that she wanted to curse because she felt angry, left out, and disappointed.

Breaking windows wasn't her thing. She never ran away or stole a car. Tracey practiced low-grade rebellion. She spit out words that were shocking and daring.

Tracey's vocabulary was the least of her problems. Much more important was the question of why she felt rebellious and hostile.

Some of those feelings are normal for all of us. We might be surprised to learn which people curse under their breath.

More helpful than cursing would be a chance to discuss our anger with someone else. Talking about it actually works to reduce our anger—especially if we talk to the person who causes the anger.

God hates to see anger get out of hand. Smart people take care of it while it is still low-grade rebellion.

A fool gives full vent to his anger, but a wise man keeps himself under control.

Proverbs 29:11

# ✯ Elevator Surfing ✯

After a few too many drinks some college students seem willing to try anything. Recently a number of young people took up the deadly sport of riding on the outside of elevators.

The object was to stop the elevator and climb up on top, through the lid in the ceiling. The students then rode down while standing on top.

If that sounds like an innocent prank, it is terribly dangerous. One boy slipped and fell sixteen stories to his death.

Too much alcohol turns us into fools who often hurt ourselves and others. Warnings don't seem to stop most young people. Scary stories don't slow them down. Maybe healthy self-respect is the best way for people to fight the terrors of alcohol.

Wine is a mocker and beer a brawler; whoever is led astray by them is not wise.

Proverbs 20:1

# ★ The Time to Believe ★

A huge number of people become Christians while they are teenagers. Young people are open, curious, seeking, and feel a need for help. Far from being godless, they often look for the satisfaction that only God can give. It isn't accurate to say that teenagers want nothing to do with Christ. Many are afraid to accept him into their lives, but they do see the need.

The people less likely to become Christians are the middle-aged and elderly. Too often they have grown set in their ways. Some are burdened with the difficulties of life; more than a few have become bitter.

Older folks are frequently closed to change in their lives. They have rejected Jesus Christ, and they are willing to take their chances the rest of the way. Pride is a big factor, as it is with all of us. To ask God for forgiveness after decades of ignoring him is terribly hard.

Like clay, we are pliable and workable at first. After we sit for a while we become crusted and dry and difficult to manage.

Youth is the best time to become a Christian. Never will the situation be better.

Remember your Creator in the days of your youth, before the days of trouble come and the years approach when you will say, "I find no pleasure in them."

Ecclesiastes 12:1

# ⭐ **Freedom Is Scary** ⭐

No one was going to tell *him* what to do. Todd wanted the freedom to do anything he chose without parents or teachers or police or anyone controlling his life.

He wasn't much different from most teenagers. To prove how independent he was, Todd drank a lot, lied a little, and cheated some. It made sense to him. Todd was showing how much he was his own person.

All of us want freedom. But what good is freedom if it leads us to slavery? If alcohol becomes our master, if lying becomes our boss, if lawlessness controls our lives, how can anyone call that freedom?

A freedom "to be me" begins in Jesus Christ. When we give our life to him, Christ helps us keep the "ugly" masters away. If we are slaves to sex, we aren't free, even though we call that freedom. If drugs control our heads, what kind of independence is that? If AIDS or herpes or syphilis wrecks our bodies, can we call that freedom?

If Jesus Christ sets us free, we have the potential to be all we can be. He helps us take the chains off and begin to appreciate living.

It is for freedom that Christ has set us free. Stand firm, then, and do not let yourselves be burdened again by a yoke of slavery.

Galatians 5:1

# ★ When to Feel Proud ★

You just finished acing your history test. As you walk down the hall someone says, "How did you do?" Your first instinct is to say, "I tore it up," but naturally you don't want to sound proud, so you mumble something like, "Oh, not too bad." But inside there are fireworks exploding and flares going off. You know you did great.

When does a person cross the line from feeling confident to being proud and boastful? How do people know if they are being honest about their abilities or just bragging?

There are two types of pride. One says, "Yes, I did a good job." The other says, "I'm a cool dude, better than anybody else." Phony pride is something else altogether. If you know you are great at math, and you say, "Aw, shucks, I can barely count," that's phony pride.

Keep two guidelines in mind:

1. The fact that you did well on the history exam doesn't mean you are better than anyone else.
2. Only the gifts of God gave you any chance on the test.

Those two checkpoints say you haven't developed an ugly pride.

Be honest! You did well on the test, and you can say so, especially if asked. Also be real! God was good to you, and you aren't better than other people.

Pride only breeds quarrels. . . .

Proverbs 13:10

# ✮ Obsessed With Our Bodies ✮

Would you believe that teenage girls become depressed more than teenage boys? Would you believe that one of the major reasons they get depressed is that girls worry too much about their bodies?

Are teenage girls simply on a health kick? That might be excellent. More likely they worry constantly about their curves, their development, their height, and their weight. Some live in fear of what other girls are thinking as well as about what boys are thinking.

All of that seems understandable. Our entire society seems obsessed with the question of bodies.

The facts seem clear. When females consider their bodies too important, they are likely to head for the mental dumper. Frequently they either starve themselves or eat too much because almost their entire focus centers on the physical.

God made us complex and interesting people. We have minds and feelings and souls and abilities. If we stare at only one part of our person, we soon will lose contact with reality. God is in love with our total person.

Study English today and drink a chocolate shake—just don't drink two.

For physical training is of some value, but godliness has value for all things, holding promise for both the present life and the life to come.

1 Timothy 4:8

# ★ A Little Mistake ★

The Soviet Union sent a spacecraft racing toward Mars. Their ground computer gave direction to the vessel, and it always obeyed. Everyone working on the mission seemed excited about its obvious success.

At one point the computer sent over twenty pages of instructions to the spacecraft, but unfortunately it contained a terrible error. A single letter of one word in that lengthy message was typed incorrectly.

Normally that would be no problem, because the back-up system would correct the single-letter mistake. The unimaginable happened. The back-up system failed, and the error was not stopped.

The one letter difference told the craft to shut down its power and self-destruct. The spacecraft obeyed and "killed itself."

Too often little mistakes turn into large problems. You say something to a friend and use the wrong word. Even if you apologize, you really can't take the word back or erase it.

Couples have sex and make a little mistake. A teenager takes a car for a little ride. A teacher calls a student a little name. A child shoplifts a little toy.

Little things can make a big difference. It pays to be careful about even the small things.

Be very careful, then, how you live—not as unwise but as wise, making the most of every opportunity, because the days are evil.

Ephesians 5:15, 16

# ✯ An Empty Life ✯

The newspaper tells the story of a group of girls who were playing dare on the highway. They took turns running across the road while traffic was moving along it at high speeds. Sometimes the girls would simply jump out in front of cars, wave their hands in the air, and leap back to safety, evidently trying to frighten the drivers.

If that seems like fun, one girl didn't think so after she was hit by a car. Dodging vehicles, she was unable to stay clear of one. The car threw the girl into the air and onto the left lane of the highway.

Fortunately she lived, but the young girl sustained five broken ribs, a broken right arm, and head injuries.

Too often life is dull and meaningless. Searching for excitement, we are likely to try all kinds of dangerous and dumb pranks. Millions lead meaningless lives, and often they become thrill seekers just to find something to do with themselves. The shame is that people get hurt simply because they have nothing better to do.

Those who become the followers of Jesus Christ can find purpose in their lives. They can become involved in helping people, in serving Christ, in having fellowship with other Christians.

Believers in Jesus Christ have a great deal to live for. Life doesn't have to be meaningless.

I have seen all the things that are done under the sun; all of them are meaningless, a chasing after the wind.

Ecclesiastes 1:14

# ✭ Just the Way We Are ✭

How many things will we have to change before God will love us and accept us? Will we have to get better grades or do homework? ~~Will we have to stop cussing or stop thinking about sex?~~

God loves us exactly the way we are. If we never change anything, God will still love us.

But what if we have lied or cheated or stolen? What if our backgrounds are pretty sleazy and our reputations really stink? How much do we have to change before God will care about us?

While we were sinning, at the very moment we were doing the act, God cared what happened to us. God doesn't run away from us when we are bad.

But suppose we have hurt people. ~~Maybe we have taken sexual advantage of someone;~~ maybe we have hit a person and done serious damage to him. What if we have a dark secret that we wouldn't want anyone to find out about?

Jesus Christ didn't die for nice people who never did anything wrong. All of us are sinners. Most of us have some dark event that we are ashamed of. Christ didn't die for the supersaints. There aren't any.

Christ died to pay for our sins—no matter what kind of sins we have committed.

But God demonstrates his own love for us in this: While we were still sinners, Christ died for us.

Romans 5:8

# ☆ Being Rejected ☆

Todd felt like a fool when he hung up the phone. It had taken all the nerve he could muster to dial the number. The first three times he tried, Todd had hung up before she answered.

Finally he asked the girl of his dreams to go out for miniature golf and a pizza—the girl he thought about almost every day, the girl with the great personality and the terrific looks.

When he called, she didn't give Todd the smallest ray of hope. Something about this being a busy time of the year. *Of the year*, he thought. Talk about rejection; it was like being hit in the head with a hammer.

Todd will get over it, although he may never forget the terrible letdown. The rejection might let him understand a small slice of what Jesus Christ must feel. Christ loves a world full of people far more than Todd has ever cared for this girl. Because of his love, Christ was willing to die on a cross for our sins. He stuck his neck out, told us he loved us, and went to the cross to prove it.

The Son of God then waited for our response. Some of us accepted his love and loved him in return. Most of us, however, told him, "This is a bad time of the year," or gave some other flimsy excuse. Most of us have rejected the love of Jesus Christ.

Rejection hurts. God must feel that. But he keeps trying. He continues to love the people who reject him.

As you come to him, the living Stone—rejected by men but chosen by God and precious to him.

1 Peter 2:4

# ✮ **Unanswered Prayers** ✮

Have you ever looked back and realized that you prayed for a really dumb thing? Did you ever ask God to give you a date with a great-looking guy, and later you found out he was a scumbag? Did you then thank God that you didn't go out with the guy?

God must listen to some goofy prayers every day. Thankfully he doesn't give us everything we ask for.

Have you ever heard of someone who wanted a certain car so badly that he would do anything to get it? After he worked, scraped, and saved to get his wheels, the thing went into mechanical intensive care. He had bills coming out of his ears.

Sometimes we pray for disasters and don't know it. We even feel confused about God when he doesn't give us everything we want. Fortunately our God also knows when to hold back for our own good.

Ted complained, "All I asked God for was one summer job in California, and I didn't get it." Maybe God knew the trouble he would have gotten into that summer.

Thank God for unanswered prayers. Some of our plans

are mistakes, and God is kind enough to change our course for us.

In his heart a man plans his course, but the Lord determines his steps.

Proverbs 16:9

# ★ Dragon Breath ★

Whenever she spoke, Kelli seemed to scorch the area around her. Like a dragon, she breathed fire and turned everyone to ashes.

If she knew nice things to say about others, Kelli seemed to keep them to herself. Her idea of talking about people was to say something mean or destructive. She believed good conversation needed to be juicy, spicy, and always a bit revealing.

Some people were drawn to Dragon Breath, because they wanted to hear the latest from her fiery throat. Others were turned off by the flames and when given a choice tried to avoid old oven mouth.

A very few dared stay close, and attempted to change her conversation to more pleasant tones. It was a dangerous job, for they often got their eyebrows singed for their efforts.

God has always been concerned about the way we talk. Little tongues have a way of setting forests on fire. Even smoldering embers have been known to burn down huge buildings.

None of us should become dragon breaths. God wants us to say calming, kind, and friendly things every chance we get.

Likewise the tongue is a small part of the body, but it makes great boasts. Consider what a great forest is set on fire by a small spark.

James 3:5

# ★ Brain Garbage ★

The worst brain garbage is not dirty words or nude pictures. For whatever harm they may do, the truly serious damage is done by dumping negative thoughts and personal put-downs into our crowded craniums.

If we are in the habit of calling ourselves names like *stupid* or *dummy* or *ugly* or *boring,* we keep slopping serious garbage inside our heads. When we keep telling ourselves, "You can't do that," or "Don't try, you're only going to embarrass yourself," or "Give it up; you're just going to make a mess," we're encouraging ourselves to live in garbage.

For some of us the biggest problem isn't that others put us down. Far worse, we have taken over the job, and we put ourselves down regularly.

Another favorite form of garbage is looking at the dark

side of everything. We get into the habit of believing that something bad is always about to happen. Anxious most of the time, we are convinced that a terrible event like a car wreck or losing a loved one or loss of money or an illness is always about to spring out and jump us.

Brain garbage clogs up our thinking process. We need to ask God to help us radically change the way we think. Bring in fresh, lively, happy thoughts to push out the maggots and slush.

Finally, brothers, whatever is true, whatever is noble, whatever is right, whatever is pure, whatever is lovely, whatever is admirable—if anything is excellent or praiseworthy—think about such things.

Philippians 4:8

# ★ Don't Believe All You Hear ★

Friendships are often fragile. Each relationship calls for give-and-take, a little bit of patience, and a great deal of forgiveness. Because friends are important, they are worth holding on to. Don't allow small things to knock relationships over. Like Humpty Dumpty, they are hard to rebuild after they crash.

Rumors fly around freely about friends. "Did you hear what he said?" "Do you know what she did?" Like splinters, these rumors get under our skin and begin to aggravate us, until we can't live with them anymore.

Friendship means we are not easily swayed by the rumors we hear about a person. A friend is someone we trust, someone we tend to believe the best about. If we let rumors drive a wedge between us and that person, our friend has become separated from us. When the separation or split continues to grow, we may soon lose each other.

Since good friendships are important, the Bible tells us not to listen to rumors. Our friends are not perfect, and we can accept that; but we must not accept every wild story we hear about the people we care for.

If a rumor really bothers you, go to your friend and ask him about it. But never be quick to judge a friend simply because you heard some empty words.

A perverse man stirs up dissension, and a gossip separates close friends.

Proverbs 16:28

# ★ The Pressure to Cheat ★

If a student paid you, would you be willing to take an exam for him? Would you take an exam for a friend, simply as a favor, without accepting any money? Would you buy a term paper and hand it in as your own?

When you take a test, do you ever write the answers on your arm or on a piece of paper? Have you ever looked at your neighbor's paper while you were taking a quiz?

School administrators say that cheating in school is widespread and accepted by many students as normal. Many see it as a challenge to outsmart the teacher. Term papers are bought and sold so often that few people raise their eyebrows over the practice.

Christian young people must find it a hard temptation to resist cheating. Since few students condemn the practice, the honest students must sometimes wonder why they work so hard.

If we consider cheating no big deal, how will we spend our lives? Will we also cheat at work, on real estate deals, and even on our spouses? Honesty is at the foundation of our trustworthiness. Can others trust us, and can God trust us?

"Whoever can be trusted with very little can also be trusted with much, and whoever is dishonest with very little will also be dishonest with much."

Luke 16:10

# ★ Encouraging Words ★

A boy in the Midwest pulled a pistol out of his bag and shot another student in the head. He then turned the gun and shot himself to death.

What was the problem? The other students teased him about his appearance and called him "Chubby," because of his size. As one student said, "We didn't really have anything against him. He was just someone to pick on."

How many of us still suffer from the insults and put-downs of thoughtless friends? How many of us are still afraid to try new things, because someone always makes fun of us?

We can do better. God wants us to be the ministers of encouragement instead of put-down artists. Sometimes we feel foolish saying nice things about someone. It's as if we don't want to be caught being kindhearted or thought-ful.

Each of us has an excellent opportunity to build up others. We can say what we appreciate about another person, remind him of what his gifts and talents are. Our contri-bution to people is to help heal and strengthen them in the same way that Jesus Christ encourages us.

Therefore encourage one another and build each other up, just as in fact you are doing.

1 Thessalonians 5:11

# ✮ Disappointed ✮

When Julie's parents divorced, her father moved out of the house. He reassured Julie of his love and promised to see her often. Before long Julie discovered that it wouldn't be often. Her father called occasionally, saw her briefly on a few holidays, but was "busy" the rest of the time.

Julie had loved her father greatly, and his failure to keep

up contact was a terrible disappointment. His absence left an empty space in her heart.

Each of us will experience terrible disappointments. The death of someone we love, rejection by a friend, getting cut from a team, or a parent losing a job. The pain is real, and often we have to struggle to get over the agony.

Sometimes we may feel just as disappointed with God. There will be things we think he should have done. We prayed about it. We asked the big favor, and then we looked for God to do something. When we didn't see the change we wanted, we wondered why God let us down.

The truth is that God doesn't always make the changes we ask for. But that doesn't make him untrustworthy. He may not remove the hard times, but God always sticks with us during the hard times. He never lets us down, because he never leaves us.

". . . Then you will know that I am the Lord; those who hope in me will not be disappointed."

Isaiah 49:23

# ★ I Didn't Do Anything ★

Living on the edge had become one of Casie's favorite activities. When the family was scheduled to leave for grandmother's house at eight o'clock, Casie would lumber home around eight-thirty. Her parents would scold her for being late, and her only reply would be, "I didn't do anything."

It was one of those habits we get into. If Casie gave some smart-aleck answer to a teacher, and the teacher complained, the teenager's reply was the same song, same verse, "I didn't do anything."

Casie had sunk into a blue funk in which she didn't care about anything, and nobody was going to tell her what to do. In her own eyes she chose to see nothing wrong with anything that she said or did. She had begun to see her behavior as just fine, while seeing everyone else as a problem.

Sometimes when we get like that (and most of us get like that), we really can't see what we are doing. But more often we know how rude and self-centered we have become.

God is always aware of when you are confused and when you simply choose to be a pain. And God would encourage you to snap out of it.

All a man's ways seem innocent to him, but motives are weighed by the Lord.

Proverbs 16:2

# ★ Lying Is Popular ★

Is it true that most of us lie? According to some reports we lie regularly to our families as well as to our friends. Has lying become so common that we expect to lie and we expect to be lied to, even by the people we love?

What does so much lying mean?

Are we afraid to tell the truth?
Do we care little for people?
Is honesty considered foolish?
Are we terribly insecure?
Would we do anything to get ahead?

The matter is only made worse when people we respect lie. Parents, politicians, businesspeople, entertainers all seem to lie sometimes, and their betrayal of truth only makes lying more acceptable.

Try to imagine a God who lies. He would tell us he loved us, but in fact he would hate the lot of us. He would say he has forgiven our sins, but in reality he could hardly wait to get even. God would tell us about a heaven, when actually there was no such place.

What if there were no truth?

Fortunately God is dependable, reliable, and *never* would tell a lie.

God did this so that, by two unchangeable things in which it is impossible for God to lie, we who have fled to take hold of the hope offered to us may be greatly encouraged.

Hebrews 6:18

# ★ Examples to Follow ★

When Mike was sixteen years old, he went to camp for the first time. During that week he enjoyed water battles, canoe races, horseback riding, and obstacle courses. Mike would always look back at that time as one of the great experiences of his life.

Camp meant more than just enjoying games; Mike also met a great counselor. A junior in college, Dave was a friendly, caring person. He took the time to explain things; he was patient when the campers had questions, and he knew when to horse around.

The camp had a terrific speaker, but the sessions weren't important to Mike. He doesn't even remember the lessons. But Mike remembers the counselor and the great example he set.

Each of us has an excellent example or two whom we remember well: a teacher, an older brother, a recreation director, a parent who made us feel good about ourselves and even about life. We can also think of times when we tried to be solid examples to someone else, because we knew how important that was.

We call these people role models, and finding the right ones and rejecting the wrong ones becomes tremendously important.

We become good examples as we follow the example of Jesus Christ. Good role models are humble, loving, and caring. Those are the people we look for, and hopefully those are the people we become.

Follow my example, as I follow the example of Christ.

1 Corinthians 11:1

# ★ Sleazy People ★

Do you know someone who can't be trusted? The kind of person who is always trying to get away with something or work an angle? He never seems to be straightforward and honest.

He's the kind of person who half promises something and then tries to wriggle out of it. Someone who says he will pay you back the $1.50 he borrowed but is a week late and only has $1.25. A person who asks to borrow your tape but takes your tape recorder, too. People deceive and push the boundaries all over.

Can you imagine a teenager making a promise and then saying he had his fingers crossed? He acts like a first-grader. Afraid to be open and direct, he looks for ways to fool people and take advantage of them. Then he laughs at the person he deceived.

Christians don't have to sink to this level. Sleazy people can't be trusted because they are continuously out to trick somebody. God must be annoyed at people who live by deception.

A scoundrel and villain, who goes about with a corrupt mouth, who winks with his eye, signals with his feet and motions with his fingers, who plots evil with deceit in his heart—he always stirs up dissension.

Proverbs 6:12–14

# ★ Prisoners of Hope ★

How do you feel when you do poorly on a test? You expected to do well. You studied, kept notes, read the material, and memorized the facts. But somehow social studies never came together for you. You still don't know what the main export is in Norway or why the population of North Dakota is dropping.

No doubt you tried. You could have tried harder, but you did give it a decent shot. *What's the point,* you wonder. *I'll have the same trouble with the next test, too.* Coffee production and how many cars are shipped to Guam just isn't your bag.

But you need that class. Somehow you need to dust off those books again and try to grasp the facts and the trends. The courage will come. You can ask God to help your attitude and clear your mind. There is hope for people who refuse to quit.

You may never be professor of sociology at Thunder Tech, but you might be surprised how much you can learn. The potential of God makes us prisoners of hope. Hope will not set us free. We must dream and reach and climb, because God gives us courage.

Return to your fortress, O prisoners of hope; even now I announce that I will restore twice as much to you.

Zechariah 9:12

# ✭ Is It Worth It? ✭

When most of our friends reject Jesus Christ, when the majority of people live any way they want to, when we are often treated like dopes because we believe, do you ever wonder if it is worth it to be a Christian?

Mood swings are common, even among Christians. Some days we ride the waves and stay on top very well. Other times the waves crash over our heads, and we feel soaked and washed out. On the days when we seem overwhelmed and discouraged, we need to commit the day to Christ and ask him to hold on to us through the storm. Storms don't last, and soon we will be back up on top again. We believe that our faith helps see us through the tough times.

The apostle Paul had some serious mood swings. Despite his powerful faith, there were days when it didn't click. He went through the motions of prayer and believing and committing to God, and still he felt like oatmeal. Basically we all go through the same experiences.

Paul found it helpful, in down times, to keep his eye on

the goal and to press on nevertheless. Our life in Christ is too valuable to simply discard because of some setbacks. We press on in our faith in Jesus Christ because, in the total picture, following him gives life its goal and purpose.

. . . Forgetting what is behind and straining toward what is ahead, I press on toward the goal to win the prize for which God has called me heavenward in Christ Jesus.

Philippians 3:13, 14

# ★ Cleaning Gutters ★

Saturdays were great days to make money, and Sean needed money. He had started to date occasionally, and anytime he could get the car, he had to put gas in the tank. Any extra clothes he wanted also came out of his pocket.

In the fall Sean and Tom decided to clean house gutters. Tom's dad had a long ladder, and they ran a small ad in the local shopper. Before long they had eight customers. They borrowed Tom's dad's old pickup and chugged around town, working at their new business.

At first they were a bit clumsy. They had trouble extending the gigantic ladder, and they were nervous climbing two stories. But by the third house the new partners were getting good at their job.

"That's a wrap," declared Tom as he grabbed one end of the ladder. "Let's get out of here."

"We haven't cleaned the gutters in the back of the house," Sean reminded him.

"Are you kidding? There's nobody home. Besides, you saw how clean the front gutters were." Tom tugged at his end of the ladder. "Nobody's going to know."

"Hey, man," Sean objected. "If I get paid for both sides of the house, I do both sides."

Sean, the Christian, pulled his end of the ladder toward the back of the house. Just as firmly, Tom pulled his end of the ladder toward the truck.

Do not be yoked together with unbelievers. . . .

2 Corinthians 6:14

## ✭ **Everyone Is Gifted** ✭

In our local school system there is a special program for "gifted" students. Because of an excellent organization headed by dedicated teachers, the students have extra learning experiences and compete against other groups. These young people have been singled out for their abilities.

We shouldn't forget that God has a program for gifted students of his own. When we become Christians, God gives us special gifts, which we can use to help others.

A Christian might be given a special gift to counsel. He might be able to lead or teach or organize or comfort those in emotional or physical pain. Someone might have a gift of evangelism—or sing anything else that God wants to do.

In the academic sense some of us are more gifted than others, but in the spiritual sense all Christians are gifted. We simply aren't all gifted in the same way.

How do we find out what our gifts are? Where is the great computer in the sky that prints out our profiles and tells us what strengths and abilities we have? We could dry up and blow away, waiting for this imaginary paper.

The best way to discover your gifts may be by trying them out. Practice helping or teaching or counseling or whatever interests you. By experience and prayer look for the ways that God wants to use you.

Your ability is there, because every Christian is gifted.

There are different kinds of gifts, but the same Spirit. There are different kinds of service, but the same Lord.

1 Corinthians 12:4

# ★ Today Could Be a Tough One ★

Some days you have to be with a person you don't exactly enjoy. When you meet, the air bristles with friction. Just being near that person makes you become angry and fearful. Your behavior goes goofy, and you aren't proud of yourself.

Here is a thought on how you might change the situation. Ask God to help you send rays of love toward this person. You don't have to hug and kiss him. Ask God to give you a relaxed, caring attitude toward that individual. Stop sending bristles toward him, and there is a better chance that he will stop hurling darts at you.

Do everything in love.

1 Corinthians 16:14

# ★ How to Be a Dork ★

The Sorenson family sat in the living room, watching television. Dad was comfortably parked in his lounger, with the remote control firmly in hand. Mother was thumbing through a magazine while ten-year-old Chris stared at his favorite show.

Jeff, the fourteen-year-old, spoke. "We learned in youth group that there is too much sex on TV."

No one replied.

"Are you putting on weight, Dad?" Jeff blurted out. "You know what the Bible says about taking care of the old body." Jeff chuckled. His father glanced at him and went back to his show.

Jeff fidgeted with his fingers for a moment. He then ventured another thought. "You guys tithe? Everybody ought to give ten percent. Boy, I know I would," Jeff continued as he slouched back on the couch.

"That's nice, Son," Mother replied without looking up.

"Lance's dad and mom are leading a Bible study. They're right in the thick of discipleship. Discipleship, that's where it is," Jeff insisted.

"Oh, brother," Chris exhaled.

"When I have a home, it's going to be spiritual," Jeff announced. "Yep, you can bet on that."

"Well," Mr. Sorenson said gruffly, "until you get a better set of parents, I guess we will have to do."

"What did I say?" Jeff's voice rose.

"Hey," Chris whispered. "Don't be a dork."

Honor your father and your mother. . . .

Exodus 20:12

# ★ **Teenagers Have It Hard** ★

No doubt about it. There is more pressure on teenagers today than there used to be. We can come up with many ways young people have it rougher than their parents had it. More alcohol is available, more pornography, drugs, mobility, more expendable cash, and more freedom. Some of those are helpful, but at the same time they can carry a terrible sting.

But don't feel sorry for yourself. One thing hasn't changed. If a young person decides to fight a temptation, God gives him or her added strength to battle back. God guarantees us that he will keep us from any temptation we cannot resist. That gives us hope in a world that is sometimes crazy.

No temptation has seized you except what is common to man. And God is faithful; he will not let you be tempted beyond what you can bear. But when you are tempted, he will also provide a way out so that you can stand up under it.

1 Corinthians 10:13

# ★ **Special Mail** ★

Today I received a bunch of junk mail. Almost every day something strange comes through the post office. Bongo Bill's is having a sale on drumsticks, or a flyer announces thirteen yodeling lessons. Sprinkled among the amazing offers is a phone bill or a postcard inviting me to a plastic pot and plate party.

You always hope for a piece of exciting mail, but most days it doesn't come. Just another pile to fill your trash basket.

But let's pretend today will be different. Suppose you received a letter with your name on it. The envelope looked impressive, so you gave it a shot and tore it open. You would feel pretty funny to find out God had sent you a special letter. You'd read right through it, eager to find out what God had to say.

That's exactly the way we should look at the Bible. It is a series of letters God sent to us. He wants us to read them, learn about God, and follow him.

No big guilt trip, no collection of stories for people who lived long ago and far away—the Bible is special mail that God sent to us personally.

All Scripture is God-breathed and is useful for teaching, rebuking, correcting and training in righteousness, so that the man of God may be thoroughly equipped for every good work.

2 Timothy 3:16, 17

# ⭐ When You've Been ⭐ Done Dirty

Derrick was sitting at the lunch table, and everyone knew he was fuming. His face was red, his jaw tight as steel, and his eyebrows pointed in toward his nose.

"What in the world's got you?" Nate asked as he put his tray on the table.

"Hey, chill out, man," Kevin dropped his lunch bag and opened it.

Motionless, Derrick stared at his burger and fries. The morning had gone badly. Brent had taken Derrick's homework and run off with it. He had chased Brent down the hall until the thief dropped his papers and kept running. All that made Derrick late for class. That was an hour ago, and he was still uptight.

"What happened, your gerbil die?" Kevin pressed for a response.

*I can't stay this way,* Derrick reminded himself. *If I stay mad, it's just going to wreck my day.* His forehead started to relax, and his eyebrows opened up.

"Hey, look," said Nate. "There's life in this zombie."

*Besides, if God can forgive me, I ought to give creepy Brent a fair shot.* Derrick let one cheek slide back into a grin.

"It's a miracle," Kevin kidded. "The great crater face is coming alive."

*God loves me when I do dumb things.* Derrick looked amused at the thought.

"Anyone want to trade a candy bar for a meat loaf sandwich?" asked Derrick. And all three broke into laughter.

Hatred stirs up dissension, but love covers over all wrongs.

Proverbs 10:12

# ★ **What Goes Around** ★

There is a popular saying, "What goes around comes around." It means that people who cause trouble will usually get hurt with the same kind of trouble themselves. A similar saying is "People who look for trouble usually find it."

Never envy people who are always causing and getting into trouble. For a while it looks as if they are having fun.

They do some crazy things; they get away with some things they shouldn't, and for a while it looks as if troublemakers have their own way.

But those who stir up trouble are asking for trouble. Eventually trouble will back up on them, and they may get hurt.

The Bible has a clever way of saying it. The book of Proverbs says that people who dig a hole often fall into it. The same verse says that those who get a boulder rolling are often run over by that same boulder.

On some dull evening it will sound like fun to go out and stir up a little chaos. You may want to grab some excitement by seeing what you can get away with. But remember, if we throw rocks up in the air, the rocks have to fall.

If a man digs a pit, he will fall into it; if a man rolls a stone, it will roll back on him.

Proverbs 26:27

# ★ The Will of God ★

Finding the will of God is big business. Many Christian young people seem frantic over five decisions they need to make:

1. Is this the person for me?
2. Which college should I go to?
3. Should I go into full-time Christian service?
4. Which career should I choose?
5. Where should I live?

Speakers seem to have special formulas on how to find God's will for your life. They tell us how to make lists, how to pray over them, and what signs to expect from God.

That may be fine. And then again it may not.

Let's begin with the basics. God has told us his will: to love God and love our neighbor. That's the starting place. It's a full-time job for most of us.

Maybe if we begin here and work hard at it, God will take care of showing us how to live the rest of our lives.

There is a secret formula and it is in the Word of God and Jesus Christ said it. Some of us are asking God if we should be astrophysicists and missing the big question: How do we love God and our neighbor?

Love the Lord your God with all your heart and with all your soul and with all your mind and with all your strength. The second [commandment] is this: "Love your neighbor as yourself." There is no commandment greater than these.

Mark 12:30, 31

# ★ **Getting Even** ★

All of us are done dirty sometime. Someone breaks a promise, tells a lie about us, or even cheats. The big temptation is to get him back. But the Bible tells us not to get even.

"Do not say, 'I'll do to him as he has done to me; I'll pay that man back for what he did' " (Proverbs 24:29).

If anyone is to seek revenge, let it be God. Revenge is not the Christian way.

"Do not take revenge, my friends, but leave room for God's wrath, for it is written: 'It is mine to avenge; I will repay,' says the Lord" (Romans 12:19).

No matter how other people treat us, Jesus Christ has taught us to deal with them the same way we would like to be treated. It's called the Golden Rule.

So in everything, do to others what you would have them do to you, for this sums up the Law and the Prophets.

Matthew 7:12

# ✭ Are You a Pigeon? ✭

This may not be the most pressing question in your life, but give yourself the pigeon test. Do you eat peanuts off the ground? Do you make a cooing sound? Can you fly up and perch on the nose of a General Atwater monument? Do you find yourself winking and flirting with pigeons of the opposite sex?

If your answer to all of these is no (and we sincerely hope it is), you have little reason to believe you are of the Columbiformes order of birds. Hopefully you feel relieved.

Let's ask a second question: Are you a Christian? Give yourself the Christian test.

1. *Do you agree that you are a sinner?* That is, do you do things that are wrong? Do you ever hurt people or disobey God? You probably won't have any trouble answering this one.

2. *Do you believe Jesus Christ died for your sins?* Since you and I could not pay for our sins, the Son of God paid for them on the cross.

3. *Do you accept that payment as forgiveness for your sins?* You didn't just hear about Christ's death, but you believe it and want that to pay for your personal sins.

4. *Do you see a change in your life?* Now that you believe, do you try to do what God wants you to do? Do you try to do less of what is wrong and more of what is right?

These are the marks of Christians. If you are one, you begin to act like one.

Therefore, if anyone is in Christ, he is a new creation; the old has gone, the new has come!

2 Corinthians 5:17

# ☆ Who Made Us Judge? ☆

There was a lady with two hungry children and no good way to feed them. Her husband had left her and never bothered to send support. Every day was hard for this woman and her family.

If you met her, you might not like some of her friends. You certainly wouldn't care for her living conditions, and a couple of her habits would probably turn you off. She has had it rough, and it shows.

At first you think you know exactly what she needs. If you could get her to change three or four things, this young mother could improve her life instantly. Why doesn't she clean this place up and get some new clothes and tell her gruff friend to stay away?

She obviously is doing some things wrong, and you figure someone needs to tell her that.

Then the words of Christ come drifting back. He taught us to help but not to judge. Our job is to serve others, not to run their lives. His words help us. They slow us down from becoming proud and bossy.

We are encouraged to take the judge's robes off and put on a servant's apron. Christians always function better that way.

"Do not judge, or you too will be judged."

Matthew 7:1

## ☆ **Good FAX Machine** ☆

If God had a FAX machine, it would be the Holy Spirit. When God wants to get a quick message into your brain, he bypasses the usual methods of communication and simply has his Spirit speak to you.

The Spirit might say, "That's wrong, Cindy; get out of there," and you can hear the message loud, like a cannon shot. You might also hear, "Go for it, Brad; help that person." The FAX machine sends both kinds of messages: stop and go.

Every Christian is plugged in, because the Holy Spirit lives in us. Our job is to keep the lines open. We stay close enough to God so we won't miss any messages.

"But when he, the Spirit of truth, comes, he will guide you into all truth."

John 16:13

# ★ **Hurting Others** ★

When we become believers in Jesus Christ, we have made peace with God. We accept the fact that we are sinners in need of a Savior. Asking Christ into our lives gives us a solid relationship with God.

All this sounds great, and it is. However, God then expects us to change the way we treat people. Christians cannot choose to hurt others, if they can avoid hurting them. To hurt people we don't have to hurt is evil.

If we cheat others or lie about them or try to wreck their reputations by spreading gossip, we are committing evil. Christians are taught to love others and not to bring pain into their lives.

In some cases criminals must be locked up, or drug addicts must be confined. Murderers must be stopped; thieves must be caught. We all understand this. But whenever we hurt someone simply because we think we can get away with it or hurt someone to cheat him or hurt someone just to cause pain, we are dead wrong.

Jesus Christ taught us to love God, and he also taught us to love people.

". . .'Love the Lord your God with all your heart and with all your soul and with all your mind.' This is the first and greatest commandment. And the second is like it: 'Love your neighbor as yourself.' "

Matthew 22:37–39

# ☆ The Cure for Grumpiness ☆

Some days all of us are little Sara Sourpuss. Nothing is fair, nothing is right, nothing is fun, nothing is even interesting. As we drag through the day everyone around us can tell we are barely surviving.

On days like that, what can we do to pick up our chins, lift our spirits, and find the missing smiles? If we make one simple decision, the day could turn totally around.

The decision is to begin praising God—not necessarily to praise God for things we don't like. We can start off with:

> Praise God for forgiveness.
> Praise God for freedom.
> Praise God for health.
> Praise God for fun.
> Praise God for friends.
> Praise God for hope.
> Praise God for faith.
> Praise God for energy.
> Praise God for weekends.

The list goes on in any direction we want. Praise opens the door of communication with God, even when we don't feel like it. Praise gets our eyes off ourselves and lets us look around. Praise turns us from despair to gratitude. Simple, direct praise can change the entire day.

Praise the Lord. . . .

Psalm 149:1

# ★ Teflon Teenagers ★

A man who researches young people came up with the term *Teflon teenagers*. They are the ones who never let responsibility stick to them. Whenever they do something wrong, they insist it wasn't their fault.

If they drink, they say it's the fault of their friends, teachers, parents, or the police. When their homework isn't finished, they claim it was a dumb assignment; they couldn't find any paper; or the class doesn't matter anyway.

Teflon teenagers often hurt themselves, sometimes severely, while they blame everyone else for their problems. They get hooked on drugs, drop out of school, lose their jobs, lose their licenses, and keep saying, "It wasn't my fault."

We do get some bad breaks in life: child abuse, alcoholic parents, a death in the family, bankruptcy, cancer, all kinds of garbage. But we still need to handle a kick in the head in the best way we can. In most situations we have to be responsible how we react.

*Accountability* is a good word. It means that when life does us dirty, we *try* to make the best of it.

So then, each of us will give an account of himself to God.

Romans 14:12

# ✵ A Story in the Stars ✵

Do you have a friend, a grandparent, a parent, or other relative who has died? Maybe she was a Christian and you look forward to seeing her again in heaven. Do you ever wonder what she will look like? Will she have a physical body, can you shake hands with her or put your arm around her shoulders? Or will she have a spiritual body, like something we have never seen?

That's a tough one and we probably can't answer it exactly.

The Bible discusses it this way. We are told to look for the answer in the stars. There are at least 200 quintillion of these glowing wonders that God made. One star is so large that it would fill the space between the earth and the sun.

If God can create this many stars with this much variety, he won't have any trouble making unique bodies for us to use in heaven. When we see our grandparents in the next life, we will be amazed at what kind of bodies God has designed.

But God gives it a body as he has determined, and to each kind of seed he gives its own body. . . .

The sun has one kind of splendor, the moon another and the stars another; and star differs from star in splendor. . . .

It is sown a natural body, it is raised a spiritual body.

1 Corinthians 15:38, 41, 44

# ⭐ **Broken Hearts** ⭐

When Chad got his class ring back, he thought the world had ended. He and Sara had gone together for nearly a year, and Chad wanted it to go on forever. Sometimes he had been a klutz, and he was often thoughtless, but Chad loved the relationship and may even have loved Sara.

She was polite enough but extremely firm when she handed him the circular symbol of going together. Shocked, bewildered, hurt, and terribly disappointed, Chad fought back the tears until he got home. Then, like a cloud that had to burst, his tears poured out, and he cried most of the night away.

Heartbreak is a good name for it. The loss is so great, the pain so deep, you can almost feel your heart break in two. Understandably you wonder if you will ever be happy again.

Fortunately God is in the heart-mending business. Over time God infuses us with hope and happiness and the will to enjoy life again. God broadens our vision and shows us there is much more to live for.

We will probably never forget the people who broke our hearts, but we do learn to accept the other joys of living. That's a gift from God.

A happy heart makes the face cheerful, but heartache crushes the spirit.

Proverbs 15:13

# ☆ Always Had an Answer ☆

If someone said, "I love her sweater," Kim would respond, "Remember, it's the inward person that counts, not the outward." When another person looked at the sky and said, "Boy, it's a beautiful day," Kim would add, "There is a place in heaven where every day is beautiful."

She meant well. Kim wanted to share her faith, let people know that Christ was real to her. Unfortunately Kim had an irritating way of sharing.

"Randy is one good-looking hunk," someone happily exclaimed.

"But don't forget," Kim chimed in, "the ways of the flesh will all pass away."

Most of the people Kim met in school tried not to talk to her. They knew that whatever they said, Kim would twist it into a little "spiritual" lesson. So they stayed away.

See if there is any offensive way in me. . . .

Psalm 139:24

# ☆ Exciting Worship ☆

Worshiping God doesn't have to be boring and dull. You don't have to fall asleep and let your head drop into the offering plate. No one has to get whiplash from nodding off and cracking his skull on the back of the pew. Worship doesn't have to drone on like a dentist's drill.

The act of worship is something we can do daily. Changing shoes in the locker room is a tribute to God, because we are there as his representative. Sharing a verse with a lost and lonely student is an acknowledgment of the love of God. Volunteering for the children's ward at the local hospital is worship in motion. Teaching at Bible camp is a form of praise to God.

Worship can be motion. When our bodies are in motion serving God, we have become living sacrifices to God. Our service to Christ is an offering that God appreciates.

Singing in a group, handing out food to the homeless, and telling children about the love of Christ all show great reverence for God.

Church services can be exciting, but the great acts of worship are the ones we perform every day as a living sacrifice.

Therefore, I urge you, brothers, in view of God's mercy, to offer your bodies as living sacrifices, holy and pleasing to God—this is your spiritual act of worship.

Romans 12:1

# ★ Good Friends ★

A group of young people were recently asked, "What are the marks of good friends?" Their answers were that friends:

1. *Are good listeners.* Friends don't talk all the time. When you want or need to say something, they are smart enough to be quiet.
2. *Have time for you.* Have you ever tried to get hold of someone, but he was always busy? After a dozen calls, you gave up and looked for someone else.
3. *Don't criticize.* They don't put us down or tell us what to do. They give advice when it's asked for, and they don't get upset if we fail to do what they say.
4. *Keep secrets.* No one wants a friend who blabs everything all over school.
5. *Accept you.* They like you the way you are. Good friends don't nag you to change.
6. *Respect your faith.* You aren't afraid to mention what you believe. They don't make fun of what's important to you.

Bad friends are a pain. Good friends make you feel good about yourself.

A friend loves at all times.

Proverbs 17:17

# ★ The Lunchroom Church ★

Your favorite place of worship may be a large church complete with a beautiful pipe organ and stained-glass windows. On the other hand you might prefer a simpler setting with plain white walls and a guitar. The singing could be traditional or classical music or a selection of peppy hymns and gospel songs.

There is no right and wrong. However we feel most comfortable expressing our gratitude toward and appreciation for God is probably excellent and acceptable to him.

That's why school lunchrooms make great places to worship. The word *worship* means "actions motivated by an attitude of respect or reverence for God." Standing in a cafeteria line, trying to decide between a taco and a submarine sandwich, may be a perfect place to show a good attitude toward God.

We thank God for the food, even if we can't name it. We relax and don't push, shove, or fight, because we know God is in control and we aren't animals at a trough. We help someone who has trouble handling his tray, because God wants us to serve others. When we settle in at a table with eight other people, we don't trash other students in our conversation, because we know everyone is created in God's image.

Our lives worship God even in the school cafeteria. The building isn't important, but attitude is.

"God is spirit, and his worshipers must worship in spirit and in truth."

John 4:24

# ★ Teenage Rebels ★

When Terri hit thirteen, she started to pull away from her parents. Since she was becoming an adult and searching for her own identity, she wanted to distance herself from her parents.

If they said it was raining, Terri wore sunglasses to ward off the sun. When her parents said there was a good show on television, Terri went to her room, for fear her parents might think she agreed with them.

It wasn't that Terri's parents were terrible people—far from it. The real problem was that this new teenager had heard it was time to rebel, so naturally she rebelled. Unfortunately Terri was rebelling against good people and an excellent situation.

Eventually the rebellious attitude got her into trouble. One night Terri stayed out late to prove she was her own person. She was caught hanging out with the wrong people at the wrong place. The police picked her up and brought her home to her humiliated parents.

Things like that happen when teenagers think they have to rebel.

An evil man is bent only on rebellion; a merciless official will be sent against him.

Proverbs 17:11

# ★ Godly Confrontation ★

Almost every time they met, Tanya had something to say about Kim's clothing. And it was never good.

Whatever top Kim wore was too colorful, too tight, too baggy, or was just like the one Karen wore. According to Tanya, Kim's skirts were too short, too long, or made her stomach stick out.

Naturally Kim didn't look forward to seeing Tanya, even though they were excellent friends and had much in common. Slowly Kim began to avoid her supercritical companion.

Unhappy to lose a friend, Kim decided to take a gigantic risk. On the way home from school Kim asked Tanya to sit down with her on a park bench. Haltingly and painfully Kim told her surprised friend about the criticism that was tearing their relationship apart.

Despite the difficulty, Kim had the courage to confront. In her case their friendship was saved and strengthened by discussing the problem up front.

The apostle Paul had a similar experience:

Even if I caused you sorrow by my letter, I do not regret it. Though I did regret it—I see that my letter hurt you, but only for a little while—yet now I am happy, not because you were made sorry, but because your sorrow led to repentance. For you became sorrowful as God intended and so were not harmed in any way by us.

2 Corinthians 7:8, 9

# ★ Good Setting ★

Youth groups seem to discuss it every other week. It's a hot topic, because young people want answers. What are they going to do with their lives? Should it be college or a trade, Christian service or secular work?

Those answers are hard to dig up. Even after a teenager thinks he knows which direction to take, before long the directions and all the rules seem to change. She starts out to be an accountant and ends up giving skiing lessons. He wants to become a jet pilot and eventually finds a job in construction.

There aren't many dependable foundations in goal setting. It's as if we stand in shifting sand, and we need to change our footing as the tide goes out.

Fortunately there is one broad goal we can all aim at and actually hit quite often. The Bible calls this goal "pleasing God." Whether we are dentists, drag racers, or pick up trash at an amusement park, we can find ways to please God. Worship, praise, service, dedication, and helping others are all close to the heart of God.

If you have a career cleaning out ashtrays at the airport, still look for ways to please God every day.

So we make it our goal to please him. . . .

2 Corinthians 5:9

# ✫ Bedtime Hummers ✫

Picture a young person lying on his back in bed, waiting to go to sleep, eyes closed gently, arms folded over his chest. Listen quietly. There is a sound pushing gently from his nose. It sounds like—it is! This young person is humming as he falls off to sleep.

Listen again. What is it that he is humming? It's a song of praise to God. He isn't fretting or complaining or cursing under his breath. He is humming about how good God has been.

Sometimes we are overwhelmed by the goodness of our loving God. We stop and drink in how much God has done for us and how much he promises to do for us, and we are extremely grateful.

The person humming on his bed may not have lost his mind after all. He may simply have accepted the facts. God is tremendously generous in supplying all our needs.

Let the saints rejoice in this honor and sing for joy on their beds.

Psalm 149:5

# ☆ Wearing Masks ☆

Can you remember a favorite Halloween mask? Did you ever have one with a huge, bumpy nose and drool coming out of its mouth? Maybe you had a bald one with red, rubbery lips.

All of us wear masks sometimes, even when we aren't trick-or-treating. When you feel like a dirt ball and your stomach is upset, your brain is clogged with cobwebs, and a headache is tearing the roof off your skull, you still manage to force a smile. That smile is your mask.

Thank God for masks. We wouldn't want people to always look the way they feel. People all around us would be wearing scrunched, twisted, growly faces.

But all of us need people who will allow us to take off our masks. Close friends are usually people we can stop pretending with. We let them see the real us from time to time.

None of us can wear a mask in front of God. At any moment he can see behind our mask and really know if our hearts are happy or sad, glad or mad.

It's risky to take off our masks. Often we are afraid to let people see who we really are. But we cannot wear a mask all the time, in front of everyone.

The apostle Paul learned to remove his mask more and more. As far as possible, he wanted his Christian friends to know exactly who he was.

You know we never used flattery, nor did we put on a mask to cover up greed—God is our witness.

1 Thessalonians 2:5

# ⭐ **Feeling Like a Worm** ⭐

Do you have some days when you feel useless and weird? Do you ever wonder what good you are or why you keep trying? Do you ever doubt that you are really a Christian and wonder why God doesn't simply give up on you? ~~Do you feel like toe jam in the tennis shoe of life?~~

Most of us feel like that once in a while. You're normal.

But even on the dark, dreary days God simply holds us in his hand. He knows everyone goes into the dumper from time to time. When we think we don't have the energy to hold on, we can simply turn it over to God, and he will hold on for us.

And Fortunately, he never lets go.

Yet I am always with you; you hold me by my right hand.

Psalm 73:23

# ✫ A Complete Change ✫

When God changes a person, he doesn't do half a job. He doesn't want us to just stop saying ugly things. God isn't happy until we start saying good things. He isn't just interested to see us stop cheating people. God wants us to turn around and begin helping people.

If we used to steal things, God doesn't merely want us to stop. He then wants us to use those same hands to work, so we can help those in need.

God doesn't have a big program designed to stop everyone from doing bad things. His goal isn't to get us all to sit on a porch and do nothing.

He doesn't want us to merely stop fighting. God wants us to help create peace so we can all stop fighting.

If we used to hit people and hurt them, God wants us to heal people and give them assistance with those same hands.

Imagine a crook who used to turn back the mileage on used-car odometers. Today God may want that same person to help widows pick out cars and make sure the vehicles are in good shape.

To stop something is only part of the process. When we begin to help others, we complete the change.

He who has been stealing must steal no longer, but must work, doing something useful with his own hands, that he may have something to share with those in need.

Ephesians 4:28

# ☆ Lay Off the Hate ☆

When we hate someone, we have a deep, burning dislike for him. It is as though there is a fire inside us. When we think of that person, the flames grow brighter, and the heat rushes to an enormously high temperature.

If we hate a person, we usually want something dreadful to happen to him. Sometimes we even want to do something terrible to him.

Hate almost always hurts me—the person who is hating. That much negative emotion often leaves me worn out and eventually can cause my stomach to burn. Hate affects my judgment. Often I do dumb things to keep hating a person. After all, hate takes a lot of work. I have to remember whom I hate and why I hate; and if I see the person, I must put on my best grouchy look to remind him how much I hate him.

Like octopus arms, hate pulls us away from God. Hate reduces our ability to love, and we must love if we are to be close to God.

Hate destroys everyone it touches. Fortunately we can ask God to help us stop hating someone. As that hate fades away the love of God is able to become brighter in a Christian life.

If anyone says, "I love God," yet hates his brother, he is a liar. For anyone who does not love his brother, whom he has seen, cannot love God, whom he has not seen.

1 John 4:20

# ★ The Trap Snaps ★

You must be glad you aren't a fish. The next worm you eat might have a hook in its belly, and in a split second you might be snapped away to become some fisherman's supper. Even when you aren't nibbling for worms, a gigantic net might sweep over you, and in an instant your minutes are numbered.

It wouldn't be much different if you were a bird. At any moment a stalking cat could leap out from behind a bush and reduce you to supper. Then, of course, there are those pesky boys with air rifles, who shoot unsuspecting birds napping on telephone wires.

Life as Homo sapiens is a great deal better, but it is still filled with unhappy surprises. On any day a car might make a wide turn, smashing into a crowd of people. A vicious virus could steal its way into your unsuspecting body.

No one can be sure what tragedy might invade his life in the next twenty-four hours. Today is a great time to live, to love, to help, to serve Jesus Christ. Tomorrow there might be a hook in the worm or a cat in the bushes.

Moreover, no man knows when his hour will come: As fish are caught in a cruel net, or birds are taken in a snare, so men are trapped by evil times that fall unexpectedly upon them.

Ecclesiastes 9:12

# ★ The Microwave Life ★

Who came up with the idea for a microwave? In minutes we have all kinds of goodies. Popcorn is popping, lunch is piping hot, tea is steaming, and leftover pizza is warmed. Push a few buttons, and everything is ready to go. Microwaves free us up to do other things like play ball and be with people. A special medal should be awarded to whatever genius came up with this speedy gadget.

Not everything is microwaveable. Some things take time to bake just right. While we usually don't like to wait, often waiting is the best possible way to go.

We may have to wait for feelings to heal. It may take time to find the right person. Normally we have to learn to trust, and that takes weeks, months, and sometimes years.

Most prayers do not come in microwaveable packages. God can answer prayer in minutes. He might even answer prayers before we ask them, but more often it takes time. But God is also worth waiting for. Over a season God may bring about an answer that only time could make.

We wait in hope for the Lord; he is our help and our shield.

Psalm 33:20

# ✫ Goofing Off ✫

It really happened just this way.

I was working as a stock boy in a grocery store when I was a teenager, and I liked to goof off a lot. One day I was with some other stock boys, and I pushed my lower lip up over my top lip and began talking funny. The other guys were laughing and egging me on.

Suddenly a customer came up behind me, and I turned toward her. Since I was on a roll, I kept my lip up and continued to make a fool of myself.

The customer spoke back to me in a good-natured way and then walked away. As the customer left I noticed that she had a cleft palate, which caused her lower lip to come up over her upper lip in the same manner that I was mimicking.

Instantly I felt like dirt. I didn't chase after her to apologize; I still wonder if I should have. But immediately I realized how much harm a fool might do.

God wants us to have a good time, even to goof off, but he also wants us to be careful not to hurt others. The mistakes of fools can do a great deal of damage.

As dead flies give perfume a bad smell, so a little folly outweighs wisdom and honor.

Ecclesiastes 10:1

# ★ In the Pits ★

Nothing else describes the feeling quite so well. You feel you have fallen into a

slimy,
deep,
dark,
dank,
ugly,
pit.

You can't get up. You even wonder if you want to get up. Your present mood is

blue,
hopeless,
useless,
grimy,
dumb.

You need someone to help you climb out of the pit and start living again. God is in the business of helping people up and out of pits. Usually the person has to want to come out. Usually he has to believe God is able to give assistance.

With those two ingredients in place, God is willing to furnish a rope to anyone in the pits and will be back to help again the next time that person falls.

He lifted me out of the slimy pit, out of the mud and mire; he set my feet on a rock and gave me a firm place to stand.

Psalm 40:2

# ✪ The Fear of Motorcycles ✪

Every one she saw was big, loud, and hard to understand. Angie was sure she could never learn to balance herself on a motorcycle and run the accelerator with her hands. There was too much to remember, too much to think about. Angie was sure she would get killed on a motorcycle.

Fortunately she had a patient cousin who took the time to explain how it worked. On a country road, away from traffic, Angie began to understand the vehicle, and soon she forgot about the noise.

Mostly we are afraid of what we don't understand. Fear goes down with familiarity and practice.

Those who are afraid of God seem to suffer from the same problem. We fear because we have not accepted the love of God. We feel that our Heavenly Father is mysterious, distant, even dangerous.

If we accept and believe in the love of God, we realize how safe he is. God is not interested in hurting people or in rejecting them. Instead he works hard at showing us his overwhelming love. That's why God sent Jesus Christ to die on the cross.

There is no fear in love. But perfect love drives out fear, because fear has to do with punishment. The man who fears is not made perfect in love.

1 John 4:18

# ☆ **There Are No Dinks!** ☆

*Why would God listen to a dink like me?* Marcia asked herself at least twice a week. As she lay awake, unable to sleep, wanting desperately to tell God about her troubles, Marcia froze at the thought of talking to God.

She felt unfit, unprepared, unworthy to even enter into a conversation with God. Consequently Marcia merely mumbled a few words and quickly tried to think about something else.

Marcia thought of herself as a "dink." In fact she frequently called herself exactly that.

If anyone stopped to think about it, the word *dink* probably comes from "dinky." It means small or insignificant. We can even feel like we are the "dinkiest," which supposedly would make us the smallest of the small.

What Marcia failed to realize was that there are no dinks in the family of God. Each of us has a special place, and we are extremely important to our Heavenly Father.

When we feel as if we are week-old bread, God remains immovable. He listens to our prayers and continues to love us each day. God knows there are no dinks.

Praise be to God, who has not rejected my prayer or withheld his love from me!

Psalm 66:20

# ☆ **Never Class President** ☆

Why would God want to work through Dawn? She has never been a cheerleader or a prom queen or a class president. Her picture has only been in the school paper once, and that was with the entire biology class on the day they received the cow brains from Omaha.

A good enough person, Dawn simply never sets the woods on fire. She generally does her homework, shows up for gym class, and sits in the fourteenth row, with her friends, at ball games.

Despite her ordinary behavior, Dawn is an extraordinary person. God is at work in her life to show his love and power. The people we pick out and call "special" are usually not the ones whom God selects. Rather, God shows himself in those who are humble, forgiving, loving, and serving. Those who clamor after the limelight are not the ones God normally blesses and uses.

The Bible says God has placed treasure in jars of clay. His love is rarely found in the fancy, highly decorated jars we might expect. That's why Christians don't have to envy others. God has given us the most important possessions in the form of his love and presence.

But we have this treasure in jars of clay to show that this all-surpassing power is from God and not from us.

2 Corinthians 4:7

# ☆ Monkeying With the Rules ☆

Do you know someone who always tries to see what he can get away with? If he borrows a few dollars and promises to pay it back, he forgets about the money until you push for it. When his parent gives him ten dollars to pay for something, he automatically keeps the change. He doesn't do homework and yet always tries to argue the teacher out of it.

You would hesitate to call him a flat-out crook, yet he is always monkeying with the rules. If a notebook is lying around the classroom, he might take it and say later that he didn't know it belonged to anyone. Stuff like that.

He lives on the edge of dishonesty. You imagine he must wake up each morning and say to himself, *Who can I take advantage of today?*

Those thoughts are impure; they are mixed with ways to get away with something—almost anything. He sees life as a place in which other people make rules and his job is to get around those rules.

The Bible does a great job of clearing up the way we think. God's word calls us to lead a fair, direct, up-front, and honest life. By reading and following the Scriptures, we learn to stop monkeying with the rules.

Discretion will protect you, and understanding will guard you.

Proverbs 2:11

# ✷ **With All Your Heart** ✷

From the top of your head to the soles of your feet, you feel tremendous praise to God. You want to praise God for:

> everlasting love
> continuous forgiveness
> steady patience

Your heart overflows with gratitude because God has given you:

> food to eat
> good friends
> daily energy

A smile sweeps across your face and you are beaming because God has:

> sent his Son
> supplied his word
> given his Spirit

This is a perfect day to thank God with all your heart.

I will praise you, O Lord my God, with all my heart; I will glorify your name forever.

Psalm 86:12

# ✯ **The Word Bird** ✯

There is a bird that flies so swiftly and so quietly, and it has never been seen by a human being. Expert bird-watchers have scoured the skies, the forests, and even the deserts in search of this elusive fowl. All their efforts have thus far proved fruitless.

Despite their inability to actually sight the bird, they have plenty of evidence that it exists. The bird perches outside windows or hovers quietly in parks. It likes to fly wherever there are people talking.

When this highly intelligent creature hears a person say something ugly or mean or malicious about another person, the word bird sweeps down at incredible speeds and steals the words. Then through some migratory instinct the word bird carries the vicious words in its beak, directly to the person who is being smeared and maligned. The word bird makes sure that the person hears the terrible things that are being said.

The next time you lean close to your friend and start to say, "Did you hear what Tammy did?" watch out. The word bird just cast an eye on you and is about to swoop down.

Do not revile the king even in your thoughts, or curse the rich in your bedroom, because a bird of the air may carry your words, and a bird on the wing may report what you say.

Ecclesiastes 10:20

# ★ Brothers and Sisters ★

Growing up with brothers, sisters, stepbrothers, and stepsisters causes a great deal of head bumping. They tend to fight over bathrooms, closet space, clothing, use of the telephone, and table manners. The only way for siblings to survive all this hand-to-hand combat is with a generous amount of forgiveness.

We all meet adult brothers and sisters who have become excellent friends and seem to enjoy one another's company. Unfortunately there are large numbers who carry friction throughout their lives.

Smart siblings learn to take out a paintbrush and cover each other with forgiveness. Most of them have to paint each other over and over again, using a wide brush and a deep, full bucket of paint.

Brothers and sisters who hold grudges travel a rough and rocky road. Too often they sink into bitterness and eventually stop seeing one another, except when it is absolutely necessary. That is usually at funerals, weddings, and family reunions—at least for a while.

God is big in the paint business. He knows that many of us are habitual troublemakers. We might change a little, but we often slide back into our inconsiderate and mean ways.

We have to cover each other with forgiveness. That's the best way for brothers and sisters to find love.

Above all, love each other deeply, because love covers over a multitude of sins.

1 Peter 4:8

# ★ Pushed Around ★

Sometimes Charlene got pushed around at school. Not that she was physically attacked, but some of the students insulted her whenever they got the chance. While Charlene was far from perfect, she didn't deserve the verbal abuse she received.

The fact that she was a Christian was hard for some to understand. When she refused to help others cheat on tests or when she avoided some parties, the other students got pretty mouthy about her actions.

All that hurt Charlene. No wallflower, she wanted to be accepted by everyone. When that didn't happen, she suffered, and usually Charlene kept it to herself.

There was only so much she could do to be accepted. Her convictions prevented her from lying or stealing. Charlene found herself repeatedly defending and befriending the minority students, and of course many people couldn't understand that.

Suffering often comes with the Christian life, and sometimes Charlene suffered for her stand. She tried to accept being pushed around as part of the will of God. Knowing that God was in it with her made the abuse worth it.

So then, those who suffer according to God's will should commit themselves to their faithful Creator and continue to do good.

1 Peter 4:19

# ✫ Secret Disciples ✫

How long can we believe in Jesus Christ and keep our beliefs a secret? How can we follow the Son of God and still act as if we don't know him?

Many of us struggle with that simple conflict. We want to live and act like non-Christians, when in our hearts we really believe in a forgiving Savior. Can a person really be a secret disciple?

Joseph of Arimathea tried it. His faith was in Christ, but he was afraid of what would happen if others found out that he was a Christian. When Jesus was crucified, Joseph discovered that he could be silent no longer. Courageously, at the risk of his own life, he went to Pilate and asked for the body of Christ, so he could bury him.

Silent, secretive disciples are caught in a terrible struggle. How can they believe something in their hearts that they are afraid to openly show?

For most of us the time comes when we can no longer be secret disciples. Maybe we will stand by a sick friend or speak out against an evil that is going on or refuse to get drunk or turn down drugs. At some point we say, "That is enough, I am a disciple of Christ."

Later, Joseph of Arimathea asked Pilate for the body of Jesus. Now Joseph was a disciple of Jesus, but secretly because he feared the Jews.

John 19:38

# ✮ No Easy Way Out ✮

The pressure at home was enormous. Lonnie felt it almost daily. Her parents were always telling her what to do. And when they weren't giving orders, her parents were arguing with each other about how to handle Lonnie.

She saw her home situation as unbearable. Lonnie had a boyfriend a few years older than she, and he wanted to marry her. The boyfriend was all right, but Lonnie knew she wasn't crazy in love with him.

But the boyfriend was her ticket out. If she married, she could jump into a new life and get her parents off her back.

Eventually Lonnie made the decision. She married a person she didn't particularly love so she could get an easy way out of a family she didn't particularly enjoy.

Lonnie isn't unique. Many who make the choice for an easy out learn to regret the decision. They later wish they had had the patience and perseverance to stick it out with their parents.

Families are filled with trials—emotions, finances, tempers, surprises—as well as the many good things. Trials and tension aren't all bad. People who stick them out usually become better individuals.

Consider it pure joy, my brothers, whenever you face trials of many kinds, because you know that the testing of your faith develops perseverance.

James 1:2, 3

# ★ Young People Serving ★

They can be seen practically everywhere: teenagers working as volunteers in hospitals, in soup kitchens, in churches, in camps, and at Special Olympics. They even travel in groups to mission fields, where they help build dining halls or houses or teach music.

Young people in trouble are more likely to make the newspapers, but for every teenager who is having a hard time, there are many more who are finding someone to help.

Slightly over half the adults in the United States are involved as volunteers. That's a large number. But almost 60 percent of teenagers report that they work regularly as volunteers.

That may not be a headline grabber, but it does tell us something about the attitude of young people. They aren't all stealing wheel covers or shooting up movie theaters. In fact very few are tearing around wrecking the community.

Service is at the heart of being a disciple of Jesus Christ. The Christian life isn't an introverted experience that allows us to sit around and count the freckles on the backs of our hands. Teenagers have heard the call to help others on this rotating planet. Christian young people have received their encouragement straight from the word of God.

For we do not preach ourselves, but Jesus Christ as Lord, and ourselves as your servants for Jesus' sake.

2 Corinthians 4:5

# ✫ Incredible Forgiveness ✫

A man drove all night to attend a parole hearing for the person who had killed his father eighteen years ago.

The parole board asked the man if he could forgive the person who had killed his father. After the hearing, he stood arm in arm with the killer and wished him the best of luck.

Growing up in a family of four children, with no father, had to be terribly tough. But somehow he could reach deep inside and forgive the person who made all that agony happen.

Forgiveness is a tricky business. Most of us have trouble letting go, after someone has hurt us. We worry about it. We fret. Sometimes we plot and try to get even.

Usually if we can't forgive we end up bringing pain to ourselves. We become bitter, can't sleep, and we continuously remind ourselves what a dirty deal someone did to us.

The heart of Christianity is forgiveness. It begins with the fact that God forgives us. Because we are forgiven, we are quick to pass that on to others. If God forgives us for lying, how can we refuse to forgive the person who lies to us?

To forgive is to lay down a heavy burden. Often it isn't easy. But forgiveness can perform miracles in our lives and in the person we forgive.

Be kind and compassionate to one another, forgiving each other, just as in Christ God forgave you.

Ephesians 4:32

# ✷ God Made You Rich ✷

Congratulations! Today you have become a wealthy person. You didn't win the lottery; your sweepstakes letter didn't pay off; and your rich uncle in Spokane didn't die. But you have become the richest student in your school, and you have tremendous reason to be happy.

God has decided to fill your life with every valuable quality you can possibly own. He has packed your treasure chest with thoughtfulness, service, dedication, love, faithfulness, and dozens of other gems. Far more important than gold, silver, or bonds, these lasting prizes are the real riches of this world.

This is hard to believe in a society that exalts big cars, big houses, and big bank accounts. But God insists these are the only enduring valuables.

Not only has God filled your strongbox to overflowing, but he would like to send more jewels your way. Before you can receive them, you must empty some of the full boxes you already have. Use your thoughtfulness, your service, your love, your faithfulness, and God will keep pouring more wealth into your treasure chest.

You will be made rich in every way so that you can be generous on every occasion, and through us your generosity will result in thanksgiving to God.

2 Corinthians 9:11

# ✬ Knock, Knock ✬

Every time she mentioned anyone's name, Sandy said something bad. It was as though she thought good news wasn't interesting enough to mention. Each phrase, each description, each word poured out some put-down of another person.

Sandy had developed a miserable habit and by now probably wasn't even aware she was doing it. Daily she played her own game of knock, knock. She knocked everyone she knew, especially those who weren't around.

Christians often have trouble with this speech defect. Their mouths, tongues, and vocal cords can't form complimentary and flattering phrases. They only deliver the uglies and the nasties.

But some Christians grow in grace and mercy to the point where they change their speech patterns. They change because they have a new heart pattern.

The game of knock, knock gives way to a new game of build, build. We look for ways to say kind and thoughtful things. We make people feel good by the great things we say about them.

Do not let any unwholesome talk come out of your mouths, but only what is helpful for building others up according to their needs, that it may benefit those who listen.

Ephesians 4:29

# ✯ Tough on Ourselves ✯

It would be hard to live with a perfectionist. Imagine someone who *always* wanted everything in exactly the right place. No pillows could be moved. Every magazine had to be in order on the table. Bottles and jars had to be lined up according to height.

Perfectionism would drive most of us crazy.

Some of the great perfectionists are teenagers. They don't look at magazines or pillows. Their rooms might even be wrecks. But when they look at themselves, many young people have no patience with their own imperfections.

Teenagers are usually their own worst critics. Every day they are upset at their hair, their complexions, their clothes, their voices, and their stereos. They slam doors, huff aloud, and grump a great deal. If someone else tries to compliment them, they feel even worse, because that person has called attention to them.

If they could, many teenagers would wave a magic wand and immediately become someone else.

God isn't nearly as critical of us as many young people are of themselves. God has great patience with us, because he loves us. We run out of patience with ourselves and want to change everything today.

The Holy Spirit cuts us some slack. He helps us to become more accepting and patient with who we are.

But the fruit of the Spirit is love, joy, peace, patience, kindness, goodness, faithfulness, gentleness and self-control. . . .

Galatians 5:22, 23

# ⭐ It's Hard to Wait ⭐

Kelly was seventeen and still waiting for her first date. Some of her friends had dated while Kelly was home chewing her nails. She felt time was running out and wanted to get on with her social life.

With Chris the problem was cars. He had his license, but his parents hardly ever let him drive. Almost daily he nagged them to hand him the keys.

Like most young people, these two want to get on with life. They're tired of hearing rusty words like "later," "patience," "just hold on," or, "tomorrow will be plenty of time." Life is exciting and unfolding, and they want it to happen now.

It's hard to wait, but try as we might, we can't have it all today. And when we try to make everything happen immediately, we often mess things up.

Some people date before they're ready, leave home too soon, drop out of school early, try alcohol before they can think it through, or rush into sex before the proper time and place. Waiting feels like a bummer, but hurrying is often a disaster.

The author of Psalm 40 was in a hurry, too. But he learned that God's timing is worth waiting for.

I waited patiently for the Lord; he turned to me and heard my cry.

Psalm 40:1

# ☆ Masquerade Parties ☆

When Jenny met him, he was sincere, accepting, and friendly. He spoke of faith and Christ and fellowship and of changing an evil, ugly world.

Before long Jenny found herself living in a closed community in a wooded area in Colorado. She was taught to cut off all contact with her parents and to pledge total allegiance to the leaders of the group. Jenny submitted herself to severe mental and even physical discipline. Soon she could no longer think for herself and had totally surrendered to a cult.

Actually Jenny had been invited by a masked man to a masquerade party. They spoke of Christ and the Bible, but they practiced mind control and manipulation and fear. Dressing up like Christians, they were merely nonbelievers at a costume ball.

Thousands of young people attend masquerade parties, believing they are real Christian fellowship.

For such men are false apostles, deceitful workmen, masquerading as apostles of Christ. And no wonder, for Satan himself masquerades as an angel of light. It is not surprising, then, if his servants masquerade as servants of righteousness. Their end will be what their actions deserve.

2 Corinthians 11:13–15

# ✪ **Plenty of Grace** ✪

Today you have to take a test, and you aren't prepared.
Today your parents are angry and upset.
Today your brother is acting like a jerk.
There are some tough things to face in the next twenty-four hours. You aren't sure how you will handle them. But God made you a promise: His grace will be sufficient. You may find added strength and courage that you didn't imagine you possessed.
Today you don't have enough money to buy new shoes.
Today you feel left out by your friends.
Today you hate to take gym class.
The pressure seems to mount, and you wonder if you can handle it all. You know you aren't alone. God is going to walk (or even run) through the day with you. He has a way of making the unbearable, bearable.
Today you feel like quitting.
Today you feel unwanted and unappreciated.
Today you feel like a fly stuck on the flypaper of life.
But God sends a message: We can get through it together.

But he said to me, "My grace is sufficient for you, for my power is made perfect in weakness."

2 Corinthians 12:9

# ★ Trash-Bag Theology ★

What happens to our sins? When we treat someone terribly or take things that don't belong to us, does God get ticked and hold it against us? If we disobey God, does he hold a grudge and wait to get even with us later?

Thousands of years ago a man named Job explained his trash-bag theology. He believed his sins were all placed in a bag, and the bag was sealed tightly and taken care of.

Try to picture God with a large, plastic trash bag. When we do something thoughtless, stupid, wrong, or evil, God picks that up and shoves it into the bag. Then God ties the bag shut with a wire twister.

Soon the trash truck comes along and hauls off the bag and whatever sins are in it. We might have trouble believing that God would stuff all of our sins in a bag and send them to the dump, but Job believed it. Thanks for telling us about that, Job; your picture helps us understand God and sin much better.

My offenses will be sealed up in a bag; you will cover over my sin.

Job 14:17

# ☆ **The Gifted Ostrich** ☆

Do you ever pout because you feel as if God didn't give you enough gifts? Do you run as slowly as a refrigerator, learn math as quickly as a brick, and sing like a rusty hinge? Have you ever felt sorry for yourself, because your hair looks like a bird's nest, your ears are large as cymbals, and your nose is crooked?

It's easy to concentrate on the things you don't like. Imagine the problems ostriches must have. Funny-looking birds, they can't fly. Instead of building real nests, they lay their eggs on the ground, like huge stones. Ostriches aren't very bright, and if danger comes, they run off in all directions.

But on a straight stretch of ground, in a race, this gangly bird can outrun the fastest horse.

Never sit around sulking over the gifts you think you missed. Pick out the ones you enjoy, and thank God for giving them to you. Pouting over what we can't do only prevents us from doing what is really important.

Yet when she spreads her feathers to run, she laughs at horse and rider.

Job 39:18

# ★ Bullfrog Believers ★

When Toni became a Christian, she changed in some amazing ways. Suddenly she was convinced that she knew more than anyone else. Her tone of voice took on a different air, she became easily critical of her friends (even of people she barely knew). Within weeks she appointed herself everyone's moral policeman, telling them how to act, what to do, and where they should go.

Accidentally Toni became a puffed-up Christian. Like a bullfrog, she swelled up and thought she was something special.

To her credit, Tony knew that Christians were supposed to see a change in their lives. What she didn't understand was that Christians should change into serving, caring, helpful, humble people and not into bullfrogs croaking about how great they are.

. . . Knowledge puffs up, but love builds up.

1 Corinthians 8:1

# ★ The Green-Eyed Monster ★

When you see someone with great clothes, does it make you:

angry,
upset,
envious?

When you see a terrific car drive past, with a teenager at the wheel, does it cause you to feel:

poor,
depressed,
deprived?

When a student seldom studies but gets great grades all the time, does your:

face turn red,
blood pressure rise,
head ache?

When you see someone with a hot date, does that make you:

mad,
jealous,
ticked off?

Jealousy is something we can turn over to Christ and ask him to help us get over it.

Therefore rid yourselves of all malice and all deceit, hypocrisy, envy, and slander of every kind.

1 Peter 2:1

# ☆ **The Delinquent Tapes** ☆

The three tapes had sat so long on Sherri's dresser that they were collecting dust. She had meant to return them to Vicky weeks ago, but then Vicky got pushy about it.

At first it was a simple matter. Sherri had borrowed the tapes and told Vicky she would return them in two weeks. After four weeks Vicky said, "Hey, I hope you're giving those tapes lots of food and water."

Now that really made Sherri mad. Vicky didn't have to be such a mouth, she figured. Why hadn't she just given Sherri a gentle reminder?

After two months the tapes were still in Sherri's room, and the girls were no longer talking to each other. Vicky decided she wouldn't talk to anyone who would steal tapes, and of course, Sherri thought anyone with a nasty attitude should have to stew for a while.

It happens. Small things turn into big things because we forget to be nice. Smart people go back quickly and make amends before a little deal turns into an ugly mess.

Fools mock at making amends for sin, but goodwill is found among the upright.

Proverbs 14:9

# ✫ A Mother's Forgiveness ✫

A young man had been murdered by a couple of people he had not even known. The killing was vicious, motivated only by hate and prejudice.

The murderers were apprehended by the police and charged. At the trial one of the men confessed to the crime and asked the boy's mother to forgive him. The mother stood up in court and said that the minute she had heard they were arrested she told the Lord that she forgave the people who killed her son.

How do we forgive someone who has committed a terrible offense against us? It isn't usually easy. But it helps if we can remember how much God in Christ has forgiven us.

Christ doesn't hold back. He is generous even to those of us who fail often. The love of Christ has long arms, which frequently wrap around us with acceptance and forgiveness.

If we have received this forgiveness and we realize its freeing power, we are much more likely to pass it on to others.

Bear with each other and forgive whatever grievances you may have against one another. Forgive as the Lord forgave you.

Colossians 3:13

# ★ Gay Bashing ★

Why would anyone want to beat up or in any way attack a gay or lesbian? Have we become so primitive and barbaric that we need to hurt people we don't agree with? It seems strange that Christians would reduce themselves to hitting and harassing others.

This isn't what Jesus Christ taught us. He told his followers to love their neighbors as they love themselves. And who is our neighbor? Anyone who is in need of a neighbor. This is what Christ explained to us in the story of the Good Samaritan.

All of us have too much evil in our own hearts to allow us to persecute others. We don't have to agree with someone in order to love him. Christians love bank robbers and murderers and all sorts of strange characters. Why would we then withdraw our love from gays and lesbians, just because we might believe they are wrong?

Does God want us as part of an ugly, shouting, hating crowd? Is that the best display of our faith and compassion? This could be an excellent day to demonstrate love to someone who doesn't know the love of Jesus Christ.

"The second is this: 'Love your neighbor as yourself.' " . . .

Mark 12:31

# ⭐ Knocking Knees ⭐

Sometimes we feel strongly that God wants us to do something. Maybe we have a conviction that we should invite someone to youth group, but we are afraid. Possibly a friend's parent has died, and we don't know what to say. What if there is a poor teenager without any friends, and we think it's time to get closer to him?

When we think God wants us to do something, our palms can get sweaty, our blood pressure pushes up on the chart, and our knees even start to knock. It's all right if all of that happens. It's okay to be nervous. There are no laws against hands shaking or even voices squeaking.

Often we go ahead and do things, even if they make us uncomfortable. God isn't ashamed of nervous people. Some of his best friends shake in their boots from time to time.

Some causes, some acts of love, some services to God are far greater than the rattling that we go through. Simply tell God, "I'm so shaky I can barely talk; but, Lord, if you'll go with me, I'll see this thing through."

Life would be dull if we never did anything daring for God. King Belshazzar became terribly nervous, but he still disobeyed God.

His face turned pale and he was so frightened that his knees knocked together and his legs gave way.

Daniel 5:6

# ✮ A Doubting Believer ✮

College was a rough experience for Deena. She had become a Christian while a sophomore in high school, and at first her enthusiasm for the faith ran extremely hot. But life on a college campus was a different story.

Separated from her church and youth group, Deena seldom found herself with other Christians. Some of her professors were openly hostile to Jesus Christ, and frequently she felt her faith was being jolted. Though still a believer, Deena sometimes wondered how strong her commitment was. She found herself doubting some of the things she had been taught in church. Deena could sense her doubts rising.

Doubt isn't unusual, even among the strongest of Christians. Faith doesn't mean we never waver. Faith doesn't mean we believe everything all the time. In fact, some doubts help us investigate our faith and in the long run make us stronger believers.

Never be shocked at doubt. Face your doubts, accept your doubts, and believe anyway. That is exactly what the father with the sick child did, and Christ honored the man's faith even though he had doubts.

Immediately the boy's father exclaimed, "I do believe; help me overcome my unbelief!"

Mark 9:24

# ✫ Christ Is My Parachute ✫

We can watch other people parachute all day long. They leap out of airplanes, free-fall for a while, and then pull a magic cord. White sheets go flying through the air and form a silky-looking umbrella.

Everything looks cool. It has to be a charge to toss yourself out and go diving toward the earth below.

We can watch parachutes open for other people all day, but we will never know what it is like until we strap one on and take a ride. How can we know if we will bail out of the plane until our time comes?

Placing our faith in Jesus Christ is much like the parachute. Watching others take a leap of faith won't work for anyone else. Eventually we must do it for ourselves.

Accepting Christ as our parachute for this life and for eternity is to trust him as our Savior.

And without faith it is impossible to please God, because anyone who comes to him must believe that he exists and that he rewards those who earnestly seek him.

Hebrews 11:6

# ⋆ **When Storms Come** ⋆

No matter how old we are, we are occasionally hit by some kind of storm. Our lives get rattled around. We have family problems, friend problems, neighbor problems, or health problems. We feel blown over, flooded out, hailed under, and rained in.

None of us is storm proof. When we think everything is going as smooth as ice cream, a sudden wind will whip up and knock our windows out.

"The storms of life" is a great phrase, because it helps us picture a terrible gale that rips over our lives, causing all kinds of havoc. Storms come when parents get divorced, when a boyfriend drops you, when your father loses his job, or when the doctor has a grim look.

Fortunately God has a way of calming storms—even the ferocious kind that threaten to tear your life off the foundation. He encourages you to lean on him and watch the winds die down. Don't panic. Don't despair. The winds will pass. The waves will subside, and God will bring you through to dry land again.

He stilled the storm to a whisper; the waves of the sea were hushed.

Psalm 107:29

# ★ Who Cut Us Off? ★

When the race began, we were excited and nervous, and the adrenaline was pumping. Only recently had we become Christians, and the new experience was exhilarating. We ran for a long time at full speed and were enjoying the challenge of the Christian life.

Then unexpectedly someone pulled beside us. We don't know where he came from. Possibly the person dashed in from the sidelines. Maybe he darted up from behind us.

As this person ran alongside, he started talking. Soon we were seriously distracted. After a few hundred yards, we weren't running as hard. Eventually we were down to a jog. Maybe we even dropped out of the race altogether.

Who was it who took us out of the race? Was it a friend who drew us away to do other things? Was it a boyfriend or a girlfriend who claimed all of our time? Was it a doubter who kept poking holes in our faith?

Whatever the cause, maybe it's time to get back into the race again. Maybe we need to reconsider that serious dedication to Jesus Christ.

You were running a good race. Who cut in on you and kept you from obeying the truth?

Galatians 5:7

# ★ Mind Control ★

Who usually has the largest brain, males or females? The answer is males. But before we get all excited about that, we should remember that brain size seems to have nothing to do with intelligence. Some highly intelligent people have had very small brains.

Most of us have about three pounds of gray matter tucked inside our skulls. A highly efficient computer, the brain not only has the ability to store and assimilate large amounts of data quickly, it also has skills to correct and control itself.

If I choose to, I can order my brain to imagine the most horrendous, gruesome murder, with most of the gory details. I also have the ability to imagine kind and loving acts of compassion in which I see myself helping all kinds of people in distress.

Unless we have serious mental damage, each of us by an act of our will can create either good or evil thoughts. In most cases we can also block off terrible plots and schemes simply by closing them out.

As sophisticated as brains are, they can be easily directed by the owner. We can command our minds to follow the Holy Spirit. Sometimes minds get tired and try to rebel, but we can order them back into line.

God gives us the desire and strength to control our minds. We must then choose to keep reasonable control.

Those who live according to the sinful nature have their minds set on what that nature desires; but those who live in accordance with the Spirit have their minds set on what the Spirit desires.

Romans 8:5

# ★ Troubled Youth ★

In a quiet, prosperous, midwestern town, the adults took a survey of their teenagers. They wanted to find out what kind of pressure teens were facing. The answers to the survey were astonishing. Just three sample questions discovered these facts:

- Over the past month 25 percent of the teenagers had carried a weapon.
- Almost 30 percent had seriously considered suicide in the past year.
- Nearly half of the teenagers had engaged in sex, with almost 10 percent having had sexual intercourse before the age of twelve.

Those findings don't necessarily suggest that the country is overrun by bad young people. But it does appear that teenagers are a tremendously troubled lot. They face rapid, unsettling change, which gives them a feeling of danger and insecurity.

There is no simple answer to these thundering problems, but one resource could be an enormous help. Jesus

Christ has offered to reduce our troubles and fears. By trusting in him we can gain purpose, forgiveness, and meaning in both this life and the next.

More teenagers need to know that they are not alone and that they can find strength by believing in the Son of God.

"Do not let your hearts be troubled. Trust in God; trust also in me."

John 14:1

# ★ Conceited Christians ★

There was a special air about Dan. He didn't walk into rooms; he seemed to strut in. In youth groups he worked hard to impress everyone with his vocabulary and his stories. Even in Bible study Dan couldn't resist saying little gems like, "I knew that," or "I've never had a problem with that, personally."

Either someone else had convinced him or Dan had persuaded himself that he was about half a quart better than anyone else. He saw his mannerisms as God-given confidence. Everyone else saw them as self-centered conceit.

The Bible teaches us that we need to walk in step with the Holy Spirit. If we walk with God, we will not become conceited. Instead, we will become humble and realize that we aren't better than anyone else—Christian or non-Christian.

One of two things could happen to Dan. Either he will fail at something (or some relationship), and he will lose his conceit, or Dan will submit himself to the filling of the Spirit, and God's Spirit will bring him into reality.

Eventually Dan will be humble. Hopefully he won't get hurt too badly in the process.

Since we live by the Spirit, let us keep in step with the Spirit. Let us not become conceited, provoking and envying each other.

Galatians 5:25, 26

# ☆ A Three-Piece Outfit ☆

Clothes are important—maybe not as crucial as we sometimes pretend, but all of us need a few basic pieces of clothing. We don't want to wear gowns or tuxedos to picnics, but neither do we want to wear rags to the White House.

The Bible isn't much of a fashion guide, but it does tell us about some pieces of clothing that all Christians should wear. Every morning while we check out our shoes, comb our hair, and select our tops, we might also ask ourselves these three questions.

1. *Are we clothed in Jesus Christ?* (Romans 13:14). Will our lives show what is going on in our hearts? Our values are different because of Christ. Other people should be able to see that.

2. *Are we clothed with compassion?* (Colossians 3:14).

Christians are alert to help others. People who are confused, lonely, sad, and seeking need us to lend a hand. Believers are famous for the ability to care.

3. *Are we clothed with humility?* (1 Peter 5:5). We are confident that Christ has paid for our sins. But are we braggers? Christians are not better than anyone else. We serve nonbelievers, and we don't look down on anyone.

It would be a shame to dress in the latest fad and forget to put on the basic clothing of a genuine Christian.

# ✯ Who's Lazy? ✯

When a girl reads a book, is she becoming cultured or simply being lazy? If a guy plays softball three nights a week, is he staying in good shape, or is he a ballpark bum? There is a difference between leisure and laziness. Sometimes we think we are getting in some recreation, while others accuse us of goofing off.

Try this difference: a person who ignores what has to be done and continuously goes after pleasure is lazy. He is addicted to leisure. His recreation is hurting him and hurting the people around him.

If we have to choose between playing tennis or putting the food in the refrigerator, and we pick up our rackets, we're being lazy. When we head for the beach without closing the windows of our apartments, we are officially deadbeats.

Recreation is not laziness. Jesus knew how to take a

break. But a pattern of leisure that causes damage is an addiction to recreation.

If a man is lazy, the rafters sag; if his hands are idle, the house leaks.

Ecclesiastes 10:18

# ★ The Outsiders ★

When Amber reached thirteen years of age, she began to feel the difference sharply. Her clothes weren't anything special, her house was quite ordinary, and her mom drove an old beater. Amber was smart enough to do the schoolwork, but her other things always made her feel like an outsider.

The teen years are probably the toughest, when it comes to appearance. A person wonders if his hair is funny looking, if his body is growing right, and if his summer shorts fit. It's serious business. Television and movies make things seem more important than they really are.

Young people feel the pressure. Hardly anyone wants to be an outsider.

Fortunately God is able to look beyond clothing, houses, and cars to see the real person. He must want us to do the same. No Christian youth group should ever reject a teenager because of appearance. Christians should never fall into the trend of labeling people as insiders and outsiders.

All of us were outsiders. We were in need of the love

and forgiveness of Jesus Christ. God accepted us into his family when we turned to him.

God didn't tell any of us, "Buy the right tennis shoes and get an expensive shirt and come back and see me."

". . . Man looks at the outward appearance, but the Lord looks at the heart."

1 Samuel 16:7

# ★ Smooth Talk ★

When someone tries to get us to do something that is wrong, he often uses clever logic. He tries to appeal to our sense of pride, our twisted intelligence, our need for acceptance, or our thirst for adventure. Like a great psychologist, he looks for the right words that will cause us to give in.

Phrases like:

"What are you, afraid?"

"Don't you ever have any fun?"

"You aren't afraid of germs, are you?"

"Everybody tries it once."

"You're too smart for it to hurt you."

And of course the always-popular saying, "Everybody does it."

The problem with these enticing sayings is that we can see through them. We know the situation is dumb, and the person trying to get us to do something is a dope. But there may be a desire inside us that wants to believe what he is saying.

If we want to try drugs, the person pushing them doesn't have to give us a fantastic argument. Almost any sentence or encouragement will get us involved. Smooth talk is easy when we want to do something wrong anyway.

With persuasive words she led him astray; she seduced him with her smooth talk.

Proverbs 7:21

# ⭐ **Lemons and Onions** ⭐

The girl must live on a diet of lemons and onions. Most of the time Holly seems to be either whining, or else her lips are wrinkled tightly, as if she just drank a citrus special.

Holly suffers from an attitude. She has declared all of life as sour, sad, and sick. Not only does she make herself miserable, but Holly has a special knack for draining everyone around her.

How responsible are we for our attitudes? The Bible seems to think we are highly responsible. We can often choose to live on lemons and onions, or we can switch to peaches and pears. We may not be able to feel perky every moment, but most of us could adjust the way we generally feel.

God teaches us to put off the old self. That's an act of the will. It says we don't want to continue with the old attitudes we have been carrying around. Second, we decide to put on the new self, which God has created for us. That is also something we are willing to accept.

Too often we are waiting for a miracle through which God will give us a new attitude. The Bible tells us we can put off the old and reach for the peaches and pears.

To be made new in the attitude of your minds; and to put on the new self, created to be like God in true righteousness and holiness.

Ephesians 4:23, 24

# ✴ Buying Big Burgers ✴

Teenagers have big bucks. Next year they will spend $80 billion. That explains why so many companies aim their advertising toward young people. They know where the money is.

Even though teenagers feel broke all the time, the fact is that a great many bucks go through their hands. And most of it is hard-earned money that the young people have worked to get. Millions of teenagers hold down part-time or even full-time jobs.

What do they do with all this bread? Most of it is donated to local fast-food places: drive-ins, drive throughs, and places to hang out. Burgers and pizza are at the top of the list. Teenagers drink gallons of soft drinks.

They also invest in health equipment like running shoes or weights. Hair care, after-shave, and cosmetics are big. Records, tapes, and videos are good ticket items.

It would also be interesting to know how much teenagers give to others. Most adults might be surprised. Fund drives at schools, coin jars in restaurants, and church offering plates are just a few of the ways they give to help others.

Giving is one way we carry out the will of God. He wants us to be generous when it comes to helping others.

Each man should give what he has decided in his heart to give, not reluctantly or under compulsion, for God loves a cheerful giver.

2 Corinthians 9:7

# ☆ **Person Under Construction** ☆

Sometimes we get disgusted with ourselves. We feel awkward, and we do dumb things, and we forget to get things done that we said we would get done.

Too often we don't like our appearance. We don't think we are smart enough, and we think we weigh too much.

Some days we can't imagine anything good about ourselves, and our attitudes crash.

Many children feel good about themselves, but their trips into the teen years are devastating. Especially girls find their sense of self-esteem hits bottom.

It's easy to forget that as Christians a huge construction project has begun on us. The foreman and head architect is Jesus Christ. Every day he is willing and able to bring about change in our lives. Christ gives us purpose, cheerfulness, love, friendship, and caring.

All our lives we will be people under construction. Never perfect, never quite completed, as in a giant cathedral, work on us goes on for decades. Sometimes the foreman has to go back and redo part of the structure, but fortunately the work goes on.

We Christians are not left alone to do the building ourselves. Occasionally we are surprised at how much progress has been made without our even noticing the change.

Being confident of this, that he who began a good work in you will carry it on to completion until the day of Christ Jesus.

Philippians 1:6

# ✭ Drinking Alone ✭

The newspapers seem filled with stories about teenagers and their famous drinking parties. We hear about groups collecting in the parks, or twenty young people taking over a house while the parents are away. Those problems are real, and many teenagers get hurt because of these drinking bouts.

But recent studies suggest an even worse problem. One

city reports that almost one-third of its teenagers drink alone. They are bored or stressed out and turn to alcohol rather than reach out to friends.

The surface problem or party problem is hard enough to handle, but when young people go undercover to drink by themselves, they can quickly become alcoholics.

Some young people laugh at the idea of Christian youth groups and "fellowship." But God knows how much people need other people, especially when those people are other Christians.

Aloneness and loneliness can drive almost any of us goofy. If we make a bottle or a can our friend, we could be facing big-time trouble. Christian friends and groups serve a great need, and every person should tie in to them.

We proclaim to you what we have seen and heard, so that you also may have fellowship with us. And our fellowship is with the Father and with his Son, Jesus Christ.

1 John 1:3

# ★ Burying Hatchets ★

Most of us can think of someone we want to get even with. The person insulted us, he cheated us, he lied about us, he did something extra dirty, and we think he should get his. More than once we have tried to think of a way to hurt that person, because he hurt us.

It's as if we were carrying hatchets around, waiting for

just the right time to plant them in scalps. We smile through the day and look pleasant enough, but we are still carrying short hatchets behind our backs.

This might be the perfect day to bury the hatchet and not bury it in a person's skull. Every day we carry the hatchet, we are just a little mean, just a little conniving, just a little cruel.

In our minds we need to dig holes in the ground, place our hatchets in the bottom, and cover them over with dirt. God did not send us into the world to split heads. He sent us to show love and forgiveness.

He who covers over an offense promotes love. . . .

Proverbs 17:9

# ☆ Don't Have to Be a Gun ☆

Whenever they passed the basketball to Steve, they knew they wouldn't get it back. Both confident and talented, Steve was a hotshot who tried to score each time he got the ball. He knew how to shoot, but he didn't seem to know much about passing.

The other team members usually gave Steve the ball because, after all, he was good. But he was also self-centered and more than a tad conceited.

Bang! Bang! Steve shot every chance he could and worked hard to make himself a star.

There are at least two kinds of stars. Those who are out to collect glory for themselves are the most aggravating type. The other kind are those who are careful to bring the rest of the team along with them.

Steve had ability, but he lacked humility. True humility looks out for others. The Christian doesn't have to be the big gun who has to be first. Humility sees life as a team sport.

That's part of what makes Jesus Christ so remarkable. He could have come to earth as top gun, but he didn't. Christ became like the rest of us in appearance and died on the cross for us. He is the star who helps everyone else on the team.

But [Jesus] made himself nothing, taking the very nature of a servant, being made in human likeness.

Philippians 2:7

# ✰ **A Gentle People** ✰

When everyone around is complaining about the teachers, the food, the homework, and smelly lockers, stay cool. Christians can be levelheaded and gentle. They don't have to fly off the handle and make ugly scenes.

When everyone else is trashing parents and making fun of them, stay mellow. Try not to say unfair things or take cheap shots just because your friends are into parent bashing. Christians can be tough, but they also can keep the light touch.

When those around you start stabbing their friends and spreading rumors about other students, back off. Slamming people and creating mischief about their reputations simply isn't our style. Followers of Christ don't have to be into people-pounding.

When everyone seems to be knocking those in authority, like principals and policemen, don't add to the confusion. Anyone can throw rocks at the people in charge. It doesn't help and only creates chaos. If there is a real problem, address it according to the rules. As a gentle people we never aim to cause havoc.

Rejoice in the Lord always. I will say it again: Rejoice! Let your gentleness be evident to all. The Lord is near.

Philippians 4:4, 5

# ★ Pray for a Teen ★

There is a teenager you may know who is making a number of hard choices today—difficult choices about drugs, alcohol, fast cars, and foolish friends. Those kinds of decisions have to be made regularly, over and over again.

The teenager you may know has to decide whether or not to have sex. The opportunity has presented itself, and as a young person your friend will find it hard to turn down.

If that teenager says yes to the temptation, a huge array of problems could come rushing in. The feelings of guilt, the sense of being used, the possibility of getting pregnant (one in ten teenage girls will get pregnant), and the even greater likelihood of disease (2.5 million teenagers will contract sexually transmitted diseases this year—some of them life-threatening ones).

Pray for that teenager. Ask God to give him or her a clear mind and the ability to make good decisions. Let him have the strength to resist temptation. Bring positive influences into her life, such as friends and books and the Holy Spirit.

The teenager you know is being pulled by an incredible force. Physical, social, and peer pressure are hard to control. Ask God to give that person a cool head under the toughest of conditions.

Submit yourselves, then, to God. Resist the devil, and he will flee from you.

James 4:7

# ☆ Abuse Is Dropping ☆

You may have prayed for it. You may have hoped with all your heart that it would happen. Today your prayers may be coming true, and it's time to thank God.

The abuse of alcohol and other drug use may be dropping. Wouldn't that be fantastic? Not that their use is about to go away. They are still prevalent in schools all over the country. But the walls are sagging, and there are cracks to be seen everywhere.

Some statistics indicate there are fewer drunken drivers. Surveys suggest less drug use among young people in certain pockets of the population. Teenagers are reporting that it is less popular to smoke or drink or to get into trouble.

If that's the case, then peer pressure to do these things is also dropping. More insiders are saying they don't need them.

The slight progress doesn't mean you stop praying, but it does mean you pause to thank God. There is improvement, movement, progress. Let's not forget to be grateful.

Let us come before him with thanksgiving. . . .

Psalm 95:2

# ★ A Room Full of Packages ★

Imagine walking into a room stacked high with presents and packages: large boxes with beautiful red ribbons; small, plain boxes with nothing but your name on them.

All that is expected of you is that you take your time opening the presents and enjoy the contents. There is no charge for them, and you are free to use each present however you choose.

As you open each box you will see some presents that are exactly what you wanted and needed. Other presents seem odd, but maybe later you will know how to use them. Many presents you may decide to give away, because you know others who could put them to better use than you can. Sometimes the gifts you enjoy the most will be precisely the ones you give away.

Such an imaginary room does exist. God is placing gifts in a room for each of his children. Some of the gifts are for today; some will be opened tomorrow; and a third pile will be opened in eternity. The gifts are part of God's unlimited imagination and boundless love.

All we need to do is be willing and keep opening the gifts.

However, as it is written: "No eye has seen, no ear has heard, no mind has conceived what God has prepared for those who love him."

1 Corinthians 2:9

# ✭ Take a Stand ✭

Picture an eight-year-old boy on top of a hill, wearing his new red baseball cap. A wind comes from the south and scoops the hat off his head and sends it tumbling across the grass. The surprised boy chases his hat, finally retrieves it, puts it on, and stomps back up to the top of the hill.

He stands there for less than a minute before another gust sweeps over the hill, snatching his hat from his head. Disgusted, he darts after the rapidly escaping cap.

A third time he forces his way up the hill. This time he pulls the hat down tightly, folds his arms, and plants his feet rigidly in the ground.

The wind swirls across the hilltop and pulls at the lightweight red cap. The hat quivers; the bill of the cap starts to turn upward. A second gust of wind roars across his head. The cap refuses to move.

Christians cannot allow themselves to be chased around by every wind that blows. When we know we are right and when we are determined to serve Christ, we stand firm, pull our hats down on our foreheads, and refuse to be shaken.

Be on guard; stand firm in the faith; be men of courage; be strong.

1 Corinthians 16:13

# ★ Other Addictions ★

If we say the word *addiction,* our minds immediately picture drug needles and alcohol bottles and packs of cigarettes. These are among the big taboos, because they do have the power to control and injure both the body and the soul.

But there are other addictions. There are serious situations that entrap us and soon take over. Anything that is harmful to us and we continue to do anyway is an addiction. It is self-destructive, and we seem to lack the power to resist it.

- Some of us are addicted to people who are not good for us. Even though they bring pain into our lives, we still stay close to them, because we think we need them.
- We might be addicted to sex. A sexual encounter is harmful, and we know it, but we continue it anyway. We are afraid to separate the relationship, even though it causes great agony and guilt.
- Exercise can be addictive. The person who is wasting away because he refuses to eat, yet he works out continuously, even though he doesn't have a weight problem, is hooked. He has passed the point of helping himself and is now inflicting damage.

If anything has a hold on us that we cannot break, that habit or practice has become our master. We can break the grip and let God be our only master.

"Everything is permissible for me"—but not everything is beneficial. "Everything is permissible for me"—but I will not be mastered by anything.

1 Corinthians 6:12

# ✯ **Remember Who?** ✯

When things got tough at home, Bob turned to a teacher at school, Mrs. Steinburg. A patient woman, she seemed to understand parent-teen conflicts and knew how to calm Bob down. She wasn't big on giving advice, but Mrs. Steinburg was a great listener. Her style was to raise questions and give Bob a level perspective.

As communication improved at home, Bob often thought of how his teacher had helped. Early one morning he even told God what a great lady she was and asked him to give her a terrific day. Later he stopped by her room and told Mrs. Steinburg how much the situation had improved.

Occasionally our memories get jarred, and a name will come back to us. God has placed some significant people in our lives at exactly the right time.

None of us would want to forget to thank God for people. Neither would we want to forget to thank them personally.

I thank my God every time I remember you.

Philippians 1:3

# ★ Here and Now! ★

Frequently teenagers are criticized because they forget to plan ahead. They live for today and often give little thought to tomorrow. Actually living for here and now may be a strength rather than a weakness.

Some of us are constantly worried about tomorrow or the next day or the next month. We have little ability to enjoy today, because we are busy sweating the future.

Jesus Christ teaches us to calm down and mellow out. No one has ever made tomorrow better by pulling his hair out today. No one has planned a better future because he developed ulcers as a teenager.

Christ taught that tomorrow's troubles will wait. Today has enough headaches without dragging in tomorrow's problems, too.

One day at a time. Work for today. Laugh for today. Tomorrow you can start all over again.

It's like having a calendar, and all you look at is what is going on tomorrow or the next day. Concentrate on today and make it the best day possible.

"Therefore do not worry about tomorrow, for tomorrow will worry about itself. Each day has enough trouble of its own."

Matthew 6:34

# ⭐ **Our Defense Attorney** ⭐

Let's pretend you were arrested and hauled into court. The charge is leaving a restaurant without paying the bill. You know you are guilty, but you aren't eager to go to jail.

Since you don't have any money, the judge appoints a lawyer to defend you. The lawyer isn't defending you because you are innocent. Everyone knows you did it. But the lawyer will argue your case before the judge anyway.

At this point you are thrilled to have a lawyer, because you hope he or she can help get your sentence reduced or, better yet, get you off altogether. Hopefully the lawyer will know what to say as well as how to say it. Your defense attorney will plead your case to the best of his or her ability.

Repeatedly you break God's rules and sin against him. You are guilty, and you know it. Fortunately you have a spiritual lawyer named Jesus Christ. The Son of God will argue your case before the divine judge, who happens to be his Father.

You would be lost in the heavenly courtroom if you didn't have a great defense attorney. In Jesus Christ you are represented by the very best. Thank God that his Son is willing to take your case.

My dear children, I write this to you so that you will not sin. But if anybody does sin, we have one who speaks to the Father in our defense—Jesus Christ, the Righteous One.

1 John 2:1

# ✰ Who Holds It Together? ✰

A Harvard professor held a seminar on creationism and the universe and came to this amazing conclusion: Something has to hold the universe together. With its vast space and enormous number of stars, planets, and other bodies and energies, it could not maintain its existence unless something held it in place.

There is a startling possibility that Jesus Christ is the miraculous force who holds the universe in its present state.

It's hard to picture Christ with Mars in one hand, Neptune in another hand, and Pluto bouncing around under his left foot. We have almost as much trouble imagining the Son of God with the universe squeezed into his clenched fist, with a galaxy oozing out past his little finger and Venus popping up beside his thumb.

Rather, the universe is made up of many components that we fail to fully understand. These moving bodies push and pull in relation to one another. Somehow, through physical powers we have yet to comprehend, Jesus Christ keeps those forces in place.

The ability of Jesus Christ is awesome to comprehend.

He is before all things, and in him all things hold together.

Colossians 1:17

# ★ Hotheads ★

He had a chip on his shoulder, and most reasonable people stayed clear of him. If someone said the wrong word to Dan or failed to say the right word, he might blow up and want to fight everyone in sight.

No one knew why Dan had a short fuse. Did he have serious trouble at home? Did he have such a poor concept of himself that he thought everyone was his enemy? How much of the problem was weak communication? Was Dan afraid to use words, so he resorted to fists to get his point across?

Inside there was a terrible rage, and it boiled close to the surface. The slightest bump, and he blew up.

Part of our relationship with Christ is aimed at reducing our hostility and anger. The presence of Christ in our lives helps us come to peace with God, with our neighbors, and with ourselves.

Too often we meet hostile Christians. They have invited Christ into their lives, but they remain angry and bitter. They have not yet allowed the peace of Christ to calm them down.

Wisdom is better than weapons of war, but one sinner destroys much good.

Ecclesiastes 9:18

# ✵ Mirror, Mirror on the Wall ✵

Every morning she stood in front of the bathroom mirror, and almost as often Robin became annoyed at herself. She saw the straggly hair and tried to give it some form. She looked disgusted at the slight trace of a line under her chin and snorted at the sight.

In her heart Robin asked each day, *Mirror, mirror on the wall, who's the fairest of them all?* And each day the answer came back, "Certainly not you, you puffy-cheeked, big-nosed bag lady."

Rarely content, the teenager left for school feeling down about her appearance. Despite a steady routine of exercise and a strict diet, Robin still had a round face—and she disliked it. Regardless of how she arranged and mixed her clothing, she usually dreaded her arrival at school.

Too much of her day was spent wishing she looked like someone else. Everyone on television was thin, the school cheerleaders all had nice hair, and Marianne didn't have a zit on her entire body.

Daily Robin flogged herself for not looking like other girls. She wasn't happy with the job God had done on her appearance, and she was irritated at the few changes she was able to make.

Robin could never know peace with the girl in the mirror until she accepted herself as the lovable child of a loving God.

A heart at peace gives life to the body, but envy rots the bones.

Proverbs 14:30

# ☆ The Yo-yo Years ☆

One day you hurry to school to see your friends, do a project, play in a game, laugh about last night's T.V. show. The next morning you drag yourself to school, feeling lonely, discouraged, a bit afraid, or filled with apprehension. Even during the day, one hour you might be excited, and the next hour you want to hide in your locker.

No matter how old we are, life seems like a yo-yo: lots of ups and downs, encouragement, discouragement, high on the mountain, then flat on the floor. The big difference for teenagers is that the yo-yo seems to go faster. Moods go flying in and out, dipping and then rising, maybe swinging half a dozen times.

Like yo-yos, teenagers ride along quietly on the bottom for a while and then suddenly snap back up to the top again. They swing out into great loops and reach new heights and just as quickly plummet back to the floor.

Fortunately God understands and is willing to ride along. Whether we are on top of the world or facedown in the canyon, God holds tight to us. He knows that mood swings are normal. God doesn't get on our case because we go into the pits from time to time.

When we feel bad, we shouldn't feel bad about feeling bad. God is patient when we are downcast, and we should be patient with ourselves.

But God, who comforts the downcast, comforted us by the coming of Titus.

2 Corinthians 7:6

# ☆ Thanksgiving Doesn't ☆ Need a Turkey

Once a year many families sit around the table and remember to be thankful. We bring out the turkey, the mashed potatoes, and the cranberry sauce. A great tradition, it reminds us of how good God has been to us and our nation.

Fortunately we don't have to wait until November when the turkey rolls around, before we can become thankful. Our basket is overflowing most of the time with all kinds of goodies—as well as terrific people in our lives.

Some of the people are terrific. They have helped us when we needed it. They have been available when we needed good listeners. They may have even helped us cut up frogs in class, when we couldn't bring ourselves to do it.

It's easy to take friends for granted. They're just around. Maybe we should thank God and pray for our friends.

And we don't have to wait for a turkey to do it.

We always thank God, the Father of our Lord Jesus Christ, when we pray for you.

Colossians 1:3

# ✓ ★ If It Ain't Broke . . . ★

Congratulations! Keep it up! Great job!

Too often all we hear is complaints. Do this better! Fix that! Change the way you do this! It seems as if we can't do anything right.

Teachers are griping. Parents are on your case. Pastors are chewing you out. The National Association to Fight Dandruff wants you to picket city hall.

Everyone is pushing or pulling or trying to get you to clean up your room.

The Bible has a beautiful verse that has no complaint in it. This passage tells the readers that they are pleasing God, and they should merely keep doing what they are doing.

What a relief. A verse of solid appreciation and encouragement. Thank God, we needed to hear that.

Finally, brothers, we instructed you how to live in order to please God, as in fact you are living. Now we ask you and urge you in the Lord Jesus to do this more and more.

1 Thessalonians 4:1

# ★ To Be Like Jesus ★

The idea of imitating Jesus Christ sounds too big even to imagine. How would we always know what to say and do? Since Jesus was perfect, there isn't much chance that any of us will get close to being like him.

Don't let the words scare you. God knows we aren't about to be perfect. If that happens, scientists will put us in glass cases and display us at the museum.

To be like Jesus, let's simply pick two areas and start there. The Bible tells us to follow the example of Christ by: (1) a life of love; (2) giving of ourselves. For now don't worry about walking on water or disappearing through doors. Let's begin with the things we can understand.

Throughout this day God wants us to show love to others. Kindness, compassion, listening, a sincere smile—those are expressions of love. He also wants us to sacrifice. This means we don't have to have our own way, and we are willing to give up things that are rightfully ours.

Jesus Christ did much more than these two things, but they are a practical place to begin. Through love and sacrifice we become a little more like our Savior.

Be imitators of God, therefore, as dearly loved children and live a life of love, just as Christ loved us and gave himself up for us as a fragrant offering and sacrifice to God.

Ephesians 5:1

# ✯ Why Satanism? ✯

They may do simple things like wearing a crucifix upside down or playing with tarot cards. Some teenagers wear T-shirts with the picture of a rock group. Others write *Satan* on walls and under bridges. The far-out ones mess around in graveyards, keep animal skulls, and mutilate dead animals.

The number of Satan worshipers is extremely small, but the news about them is shocking. A few may be seriously into soul contracts and submission to evil, but authorities say there aren't many. Most of the teenagers who dabble in Satanism seem to be rebels against society and its norms. They want to escape a society that appears to reject them. The biggest problem is that they have chosen such a poor way to stand out and be different.

There is a way to step out and be different from the unjust and often cruel world we live in. The way to escape the control of evil is to move toward Jesus Christ, not to experiment with Satan. By giving our lives to Christ, we become part of the divine nature. Piddling with Satan is empty, dead end, and sometimes dangerous.

A better life is available, but it can't be found by fooling around with the symbols of evil.

Through these he has given us his very great and precious promises, so that through them you may participate in the divine nature and escape the corruption in the world caused by evil desires.

2 Peter 1:4

# ☆ A Dollar Not to ☆ Get Pregnant

Teenage girls in Denver were collecting a dollar a day if they didn't get pregnant. Seven dollars for one week. This small amount of money gave them a hard decision to make.

The girls are often looking for purpose in life. If they have babies and become mothers, they feel a sense of being someone. They are needed, and life has meaning. On the other hand, if they take the seven dollars a week, the girls have money, and that helps them feel like people.

Either way they are looking for something to fill up the emptiness in their lives. A baby or seven bucks; it's a difficult choice for some lonely teenagers to make.

If they could be introduced to Jesus Christ, they could find many reasons to be alive. God calls us to himself and gives us purpose. We not only reach for our own goals in life, but more important, we can work to fulfill God's goals, too.

Many of us feel as if we have some missing parts. We might try to replace those parts with a boyfriend, drugs, cars, alcohol, a baby, or seven bucks. For Christians the missing parts are supplied by Jesus Christ. God has a purpose for each of us, probably several purposes. We begin understanding those by becoming one with Christ.

And we know that in all things God works for the good of those who love him, who have been called according to his purpose.

Romans 8:28

# ☆ Beautiful People ☆

We know what real beauty is. If we discuss the subject at all, we usually admit that beautiful people are the ones who are kind and gentle and loving. The size of a forehead or a nose or the shapely form of a body could never make a person beautiful.

Though we know this, we are still tempted to search for beauty on the outside. We prance in front of mirrors and look longingly through magazines, trying to understand what beauty is and who has it.

God tells us what beauty really is, and we know he is right. Ideal chins or flowing hair or dimples can't tell us if people are beautiful. A well-proportioned person who is mean and inconsiderate drips with ugliness, no matter what the outward shell looks like.

It's hard for some teenagers to accept God's concept of genuine and lasting beauty. Beauty is something that could never be shown on the cover of a magazine. A gentle and a calm spirit carries a beauty that we can never lose. God appreciates this kind of beauty, and eventually almost everyone else does, too.

Charm is deceptive, and beauty is fleeting; but a woman who fears the Lord is to be praised.

Proverbs 31:30

# ✯ Blowing Up ✯

Doyle had a great three-point shot. He would stand outside the circle and drop balls in the hoop all day. What he didn't like was to have the person guarding him fall in his face. As Doyle would shoot, the defense player would often leap into the air and come crashing down on top of him.

This may not have looked like much of a problem, because Doyle sank half his shots. But each time the rushing player fell on him, Doyle became angry and wanted to punch the guy. About the third or fourth time this happened, Doyle was furious.

Fortunately Doyle had a friend on the team named Brian. Whenever Brian saw that Doyle was losing his cool, he would hurry over and say, "It's all right, man. No harm done. Don't let him rule you."

Most of the time Brian could keep Doyle from blowing up. He simply kept an eye open and moved quickly when he could see that Doyle was steamed.

Brian was helping to carry Doyle's burden. Doyle could barely handle the pressure, and he needed someone to lighten the load. Brian did that by taking some of the steam out of his friend.

When Christians see each other overloaded, they try to jump in before their friends do something they could regret.

Carry each other's burdens, and in this way you will fulfill the law of Christ.

Galatians 6:2

# ★ The Limits of Happiness ★

All Phil wanted was to be happy. He laughed a lot, horsed around, was a great friend, and offered everyone a ride when he could.

Phil thought a person couldn't be too happy. Whatever turned him on and whatever entertained his friends, Phil was eager to try.

He thought there was almost no limit to happiness. His reputation was that Phil would try practically anything. That's why his friends liked to hang around with him. They wanted to see what fool thing he would do next.

Then, late one night, with four friends packed into the car, Phil had trouble holding the road as he tried to negotiate a turn. It wasn't the alcohol or the car or the gravel road that caused the vehicle to roll over. Behind it all was Phil's deep need to find happiness.

Happiness makes sense. We ought to get that out of life. But the search for happiness has to have limits.

Be happy, young man, while you are young, and let your heart give you joy in the days of your youth. Follow the ways of your heart and whatever your eyes see, but know that for all these things God will bring you to judgment.

Ecclesiastes 11:9

# ✮ Hard-Shell Teenagers ✮

Whatever Terri's mother said, the teenage girl immediately tried to do the opposite.

"Your stereo is awfully loud."

Terri would raise the volume.

"Have you done your homework?"

Terri would close her books.

"Hold that phone call to ten minutes."

Terri kept talking, to stretch the time to fifteen minutes.

Terri had become a hard-shell teenager. She wasn't going to let anything that her mother said stick to her. Locked in a fruitless battle, Terri refused to allow her mother to help her with anything.

Sometimes her mother did talk too much. She gave advice when it wasn't needed. She set rules that seemed to serve no purpose. But just as often Terri's mother was exactly right. Instead of admitting it and making the adjustment, Terri tried her best to ignore her mother.

Parents can be right. Too often young people hurt themselves, trying to prove their parents are wrong. They play hard-shell and refuse to let good instruction, guidance, and advice stick to them. Parents are some of God's best gifts.

Listen, my son, to your father's instruction and do not forsake your mother's teaching.

Proverbs 1:8

# ☆ Don't Follow Fools ☆

Are you ever bewildered when you see two or three people following a fool around? It happens all the time. There is some teenager who drives a car like a gorilla, but everybody piles in the car with him and tears off down the road. Another person seems to enjoy taunting teachers; he tries to get a teacher to blow up just to get under her skin.

We have a way of honoring fools as if they were geniuses. The bolder and dumber and more outrageous some people are, the more likely they seem to be to collect a following.

God warns us against chasing around after dopes. The Bible says it's like tying a stone inside a sling. You pull the sling back and aim at your target. But when you let go, the stone stays in the sling and could hit just about anything. What it is most likely to hit is the person holding the sling.

Following fools is dangerous. None of us has to apologize for giving up on someone who is obviously heading for trouble.

Like tying a stone in a sling is the giving of honor to a fool.

Proverbs 26:8

# ★ Nothing Is Impossible ★

God has the power to do anything. We understand omnipotence as being all-powerful, and God *is* omnipotent. He could make fish drown and turn birds into stone, causing them to drop from the sky.

But just because God can do all things doesn't mean he will do everything. He could turn dogs into elephants, but they would keep smashing the doghouse into splinters. That would be silly.

Just because God can doesn't mean he will or that he should.

God could make us all rich, but God knows that wealth can be extremely harmful. When we pray and ask God for a cool million a year, he may not fork it over. He doesn't think riches are as important as we do.

But what if we ask for an unselfish thing? Suppose we pray that the children in Africa be fed. God may have already answered that prayer. He has put food in the fields, made ships and trucks available; he has given Christians plenty of money to pay for it all. God has plenty of Christian farmers and technicians and scientists to teach Africans to grow crops.

Maybe God has already done the impossible by making all of these resources available. The problem could be that we don't carry out the miracle.

"For nothing is impossible with God."

Luke 1:37

161

# ★ Believe It Will Happen ★

When Linus approached his senior year in high school, he knew his grades weren't earthshaking. His odds of being accepted into a college weren't great, but Linus had recently acquired a great desire to go.

One evening he sat down and had a conversation with God. No deals. He didn't tell God that if he got into college he would promise to open a pew and pulpit store. Linus didn't promise to give his second child as a church janitor.

He simply talked it out with God. Step by step he outlined his dream and told God why he wanted it to happen. He then described what he was willing to do and what sacrifices he was willing to make.

Linus wanted God to take the faith walk with him. He didn't have all the money he needed, and he wasn't absolutely sure he could handle the classwork. Nevertheless Linus described the vision and asked God to help make it come true.

If God chose, he was free to alter the plan; Linus was careful to explain that. But all things being equal, this was the goal, and Linus believed it could happen.

Faith has the ability to make dreams come true, even when we don't know how it will happen.

Now faith is being sure of what we hope for and certain of what we do not see.

Hebrews 11:1

# ✫ One Special Day ✫

Whatever yesterday was like, it's gone into the pages of history. However we may have messed up or whatever we may have done well, either way it is completed, finished, and sealed.

Tomorrow could bring just about anything. Our bicycle seats could erupt with hundreds of maggots, the rivers could fill with giant frogs, and every pizza store could be closed by the government. Tomorrows are too unpredictable to worry about.

Today is another matter. Today is something we can get our hands on. Like wet clay we can mold today and work it with our fingers and try to make it into a work of art and fun and purpose. Today is where it is, because we can't work with tomorrow until it comes.

This day is a gift from God. Like flowers and waterfalls and angels and oceans, this day was God's idea. He gives it to us, like a present.

We can go at this day full force. We can grab it with enthusiasm, anticipation, and excitement. Today is a special present from God to us. It's time to open it and see what wonders are inside.

This is the day the Lord has made; let us rejoice and be glad in it.

Psalm 118:24

# ☆ Chasing God Away ☆

If we forget to talk to God or don't read the Bible, will God turn his back on us and walk away?

God's love for us never fails.

What if we do things that are selfish and even mean? Will God get upset at us and refuse to help?

God's love is steady as a rock.

Sometimes we don't care what God thinks. We plan our lives without him and simply live for ourselves. Doesn't God get disgusted with us?

God's love isn't fickle.

Suppose we disobey God, and we know what we are doing is dead wrong. Will God hide for a while and ignore us?

God's love isn't dependent on our behavior.

What happens when we get a lousy attitude and aren't nice to anyone and become miserable characters?

God's love sent Christ to die on the cross for nice people and also for miserable characters.

But I trust in your unfailing love; my heart rejoices in your salvation.

Psalm 13:5

# ✭ Seeing Through Us ✭

Some days I worry that God may find out all about me. I fear God will know what I am thinking, or he will learn about my evil thoughts or my selfish plans.

I might just as well relax. God already knows every petty thought and desire I have. I can go ahead and discuss every shadow in my life, because God knows what is going on inside my mind and soul.

Imagine that God has picked me up with one hand, and he holds a lamp in the other hand. Like a piece of paper, he can see right through me. He knows what blotches are there, what flaws are in the material, and any other imperfections.

I can come clean with God. I can tell him about all the weird ideas and crazy dreams and ugly inventions that go on in my heart and brain. He has already seen them through the light, and God won't be embarrassed to discuss them.

The lamp of the Lord searches the spirit of a man; it searches out his inmost being.

Proverbs 20:27

# ★ Feeling Crushed ★

Everyone gets crushed sometime. Like a soft-drink can smashed on the pavement, you feel totally bent out of shape. There are many ways to get crushed.

A boyfriend or girlfriend dumps you.

A parent moves out.

A friend drops you.

A group pushes you out.

A team manager benches you.

All kinds of people can break our hearts. Most often they are the people we care about the most—the people we felt attached to, and now they have cut off that attachment.

Sometimes it takes a few days to shake off the disappointment. We collect other interests, other friends, and we sew up the wounds. A few broken relationships never entirely heal.

God understands the brokenhearted. He has had his heart broken many times. But each time God bounces back and chooses to love again. God can be hurt, because God allows himself to feel and to love.

He is also in the business of heart healing. God reminds us what is really important, and he gives us other people to care about. He is the great counselor who shows us how to rise up and live again in spirit and in joy.

He heals the brokenhearted and binds up their wounds.

Psalm 147:3

# ★ Seaweed Head ★

It must have been lonely, lying in the dark, wet stomach of a fish. Jonah had run away from God. He had been thrown away by the sailors on the ship. The prophet was a bigoted failure who was going to die a miserable death, sitting in the gastric fluids of a monstrous sea animal.

Jonah's only hat was a swatch of wet, green seaweed, draped around his forehead. How much can one person mess up? There was a time when he received personal messages from God. He did valuable work, taking messages wherever God wanted him to go. Now he had sunk to the bottom of the belly of a fish, to serve as part of a watery meal.

It happens. All of us hit bottom sometimes. Did you ever sit on your bedroom floor, smelling your own tennis shoes? Have you ever walked home in the rain, not half caring if you drowned? Did you ever eat a jar full of cookies because you thought you were ugly?

Everybody has been in the belly of the fish. We have all felt as if someone else has swallowed us whole and spit us out again.

The good news is that God still turns seaweed heads into happy people. He still rescues us from the depths of despair and tosses us back up on dry land again. God never gives up on a seaweed head.

"The engulfing waters threatened me, the deep surrounded me; seaweed was wrapped around my head."

Jonah 2:5

# ★ Friends of Bats ★

An organization has been founded in England, with 2,000 members who want to protect bats. So many cruel and untrue stories have been told about these flying mammals that most people seem to hate and dread the little night creatures.

The fact is that not only are most bats harmless, they even do some great jobs to help people. For one thing their droppings help fertilize the soil. For another, many bats eat half their weight in bugs and insects every night. Most of us would be well off if we had a few bats racing around our backyards.

Unfortunately after centuries of gossip and a scary story about Dracula sucking blood out of people's necks, we often want to immediately kill every bat we see. Once we believe a piece of gossip, the stories can hold on for hundreds of years.

Gossip must be one of the main killers of friendships. We might drop a close friend because we heard a rumor, though we don't have any real idea of whether or not it's true.

Some people have the habit of talking about others and hurting their reputations. God wants us to stay away from people who spread rumors and lies.

Besides, they get into the habit of being idle and going from house to house. And not only do they become idlers, but also gossips and busybodies, saying things they ought not to.

1 Timothy 5:13

# ✮ **The End of the World** ✮

Scientists believe that some day a small planet called an asteroid will come racing toward the earth and collide with our planet. Possibly 500 miles across, the thunderous asteroid could knock our world off its course enough to wreck much of life as we know it.

Because they are so certain this will eventually happen, large amounts of money are spent yearly to search for this devastating asteroid. If it is seen in time, we may be able to hit it with a weapon that will send the invading planet away from ours.

Don't lose any sleep over this impending tragedy. Astronomers tell us it may be a million years before this happens. Sensible people check the skies, just in case, but none of us should pace the floor, wondering what to do next.

There is a big difference between worry and preparation. Smart people look out for the future. Worriers simply fret and wring their hands in despair.

Many of us are big-time worriers. We sweat getting married, having children, finding a home, years before we are ready. We agonize over illness and diseases just because they might happen.

Christ reminded us that no one has yet added even a day to life by worry. Look in the skies one time tonight for a gigantic asteroid and then go to bed and forget it.

"Who of you by worrying can add a single hour to his life?"

Matthew 6:27

# ✮ The Love Banquet ✮

Where is your favorite place to pig out? Do you enjoy a gigantic buffet, where you can eat all you want? Do you like plenty of variety, so you can zero in on the things you want the most, like rich desserts and gobs of meat and piles of nachos?

When you are in just the right mood, it's fun to rake through the buffet and then come back second and third times. Finally when you're sure you can't eat another bite, do you waddle over to the free ice cream machine and make yourself a sundae with hot fudge and nuts and a big red cherry? That's living.

Picture another type of buffet. You walk over to a large table, and on the table are dozens of notes, all of them addressed to you. They are personal messages from God.

One note says, "I love you exactly as you are." Another says, "You did a great job helping your friend." A third message is "When you hurt, my love pours out toward you."

You walk around the table and carefully read each note, because they are all addressed to you. And every message is directly from God.

Welcome to the love banquet. It's a feast where you can fill yourself with the expressions of God's rich love for you personally.

How great is the love the Father has lavished on us, that we should be called children of God! . . .

1 John 3:1

# ⭐ The Christian Lone Ranger ⭐

The story I heard was that the Lone Ranger was a Texas Ranger who was attacked by a gaggle of bad guys and left for dead. His fellow rangers were killed, but the Lone Ranger set out to find the rotten dudes who had done this.

He was an easy hero to admire. Tight-lipped and tough, he didn't ask for help and never gave any slack to the ruthless renegades he sought.

But even the Lone Ranger needed a companion. That's why he and his faithful Indian friend, Tonto, kept each other company.

Sometimes we think we can be Christian Lone Rangers. We imagine that we can ride through the world all by ourselves, not needing anyone else. The Christian life doesn't work well as a solo act. We desperately need one another. Totally alone, we run into situations that most of us can't handle well.

We need to tie into a Bible study, a youth group, a support group, a prayer group, or a discipleship program—something that gives us solid contact with other believers.

Too many Christians who swim alone end up drowning in a hostile world.

The eye cannot say to the hand, "I don't need you!" And the head cannot say to the feet, "I don't need you."

1 Corinthians 12:21

# ✲ Afraid to Try ✲

When Sheila walked past the theater at school, she could hear the students reading lines. Acting seemed like exciting fun to the high school sophomore. Since junior high she had watched plays, always wondering if she could do something like that.

Memorizing lines, changing expressions, emoting feelings, bringing an audience one moment to tears and the next moment to laughter; painting sets, wearing costumes, showing up early for makeup—silently Sheila wondered about these things in her heart, but she had never convinced her legs to walk up to the director and ask for a script.

Early one morning Sheila discussed her dream with God. She wasn't sure she should, but it was something that wouldn't go away. Sheila didn't ask God for a part; she simply asked him for help in asking for a book.

That afternoon, trembling but strangely confident, Sheila winked at God, and the two of them walked courageously up to the director.

God is able and willing to give us confidence when we commit our actions to him. He helps us live for him, help others, and try some of our dreams by giving us boldness even when we are afraid.

For God did not give us a spirit of timidity, but a spirit of power, of love and of self-discipline.

2 Timothy 1:7

# ✭ Living Faith ✭

How do we know if we really believe in Jesus Christ? Are we sure it isn't just some words we said but didn't mean? There are a number of ways to test our faith. It's like a small package that we use to test a battery. If we put the battery in and press down, a signal will go on that tells us if there is life in the battery.

One test of our faith is to ask if we care about others. Christ doesn't enter our hearts simply to make us self-centered. Genuine faith makes us reach out and do things that are good. This isn't the only test for a living faith, but it is an important one.

Sometimes when we feel as if our faith in Christ is dull and useless, we might look for a way to bring it back to life. Real faith does something. Weak faith is motionless and limps around. Vital faith gets out of the bean bag chair and finds something good to do. Puny faith sits around and counts freckles. Strong faith gets involved.

How can we tell if our pet cat is alive? Eventually it has to move. Christians have to move, too, and they will know they are alive.

In the same way, faith by itself, if it is not accompanied by action, is dead.

James 2:17